Getting Started With Micro Focus Personal COBOL™ for Windows

E. Reed Doke, Ph.D.
Southwest Missouri State University

John Wiley & Sons, Inc.
New York Chichester Weinheim Brisbane Singapore Toronto

ISBN 0-471-18490-X

Printed in the United States of America

10 9 8 7 6

Printed and bound by Bradford & Bigelow, Inc.

Table of Contents

Chapter 6: Additional Features of Personal COBOL

Chapter 7: File Processing

Appendix A: Troubleshooting

Appendix B: Program Listings

Index

Preface

What This Manual Is and Is Not

This manual is designed to help you install the Micro Focus Personal COBOL for Windows system and learn how to use it. This manual does not provide a comprehensive discussion of the COBOL language, the personal computer, the Windows Operating System, or Object-Oriented programming. References are provided at the appropriate places for those wishing to learn more about these topics.

This manual was written for those wishing to learn about COBOL using Personal COBOL for Windows. You may be a student in a COBOL programming class or an experienced COBOL programmer wanting to learn about the new Object-Oriented extensions to this popular language. This manual describes how to use the Micro Focus Personal COBOL for Windows system. It is intended to give you an overview of the system along with sufficient examples to enable you to begin to use the system to develop COBOL programs.

Although this system provides the tools to learn how to develop Object COBOL class programs, it is also a very powerful learning tool for developing traditional procedural (Non-OO) programs. This system provides two facilities for entering, editing and compiling programs: the Animator and the Browser. As you will see, the Browser is an important Object COBOL development tool, but we can also use it for non-OO program development.

How This Manual is Organized

This manual is designed to be used for reference once the Personal COBOL system is installed. You can select the topic of interest, and then turn directly to that section for the information. The following discusses the purpose and contents of each chapter and the appendix.

Chapter 1 provides a brief description of COBOL's history and the Micro Focus company. It is intended to give you a perspective of COBOL's evolution and to introduce you to the Micro Focus company. In addition, the Micro Focus Personal COBOL for Windows system is summarized.

Chapter 2 reviews the hardware requirements for the system and describes how to install it using either Windows 3.1 or Windows 95 operating systems. You can obviously skip this section if your system is already installed. All of the screens used in the figures, with the exception of the Windows 3.1 installation screens, were captured from a Windows 95 system. Although it is a different operating system, the appearance of the screens is very similar to those displayed in Windows 3.1.

Chapter 3 presents a summary of the Help facility, the Animator and the Browser. A simple procedural program is entered, compiled and executed, first using the Animator, and then using the Browser. This chapter is important to those wanting to enter and execute COBOL programs using either the Animator or the Browser. These two facilities are the backbone of the Personal COBOL system, and a good understanding of their features will help you as you begin your study of COBOL.

Chapter 4 describes the Animator in more detail. A simple procedural program is entered and compiled. Then the program is executed and the various debugging facilities of the system are illustrated. The Animator is explored in more detail by illustrating its various features with a real program. Those intending to learn procedural COBOL will want to go through this chapter thoroughly.

Chapter 5 introduces object-oriented (OO) programming. A small class program is developed and executed. The Browser is used to develop the sample program. This is an important chapter if your objective is to explore object-oriented programming and Object COBOL. The Browser and its facilities are illustrated using a class program written in Object COBOL.

Chapter 6 describes additional features of the Personal COBOL System. A summary of the Personal Dialog System, the Class Library, and Screen I/O is presented. This chapter does not provide an in-depth description of these features. Instead, it gives you an idea of what they are and suggests avenues for further exploration and study.

Chapter 7 describes and illustrates how to create and access sequential files using the system. In addition, the chapter illustrates how to print a report. Procedural batch programs are used to illustrate these techniques.

Appendix A discusses how to identify and resolve problems with the installation and use of the Personal COBOL System.

Appendix B contains a complete listing of the seven programs used as examples in the manual.

I want to thank the following reviewers for their valuable and constructive feedback on the manuscript: Connie Daniel, Dakota State University (who discovered far more errors than I want to admit); Al Lorents, Northern Arizona University; Emerson Maxson, Boise State University; Nancy Stern, Hofstra University. Also my special thanks go to Beth Lang Golub, Editor and David B. Kear, Assistant Editor at John Wiley & Sons for their encouragement and support.

Chapter 1

An Introduction to Micro Focus Personal COBOL

The Evolution of COBOL

The Micro Focus Company

About Micro Focus Personal COBOL for Windows

The Evolution of COBOL

Although some claim that COBOL is a dying language, evidence of its use in industry suggests otherwise. Millions of programmers use COBOL daily, and billions of lines of COBOL code exist, with millions of new lines added annually. Not only is COBOL very much alive, it is by far the most dominant language in business (Snyder, 1992).

Currently, there are over three million COBOL programmers in the world (Howard, 1993; McFarland, 1995). According to the Gartner Group, COBOL programmers represent 80 percent of all programmers in the world (McFarland, 1995). A recent study by Litecky and Arnett (1994) found that COBOL programming continues to be a highly-demanded job skill. Another study indicated that over 70 percent of all entry-level programming positions value a knowledge of COBOL (Lauer and Graf, 1994).

COBOL is the dominant programming language of the corporate world, with over 80 percent of all code written in COBOL (McFarland, 1995). Almost half of all development staffs of medium and large U.S. companies use COBOL as their primary language (Saade and Wallace, 1995), and over 70 percent of current business systems are written in COBOL (Snyder, 1992). The volume of COBOL code is growing at approximately 15 percent per year (Saade and Wallace, 1995), which translates into over 10 billion new lines of COBOL code per year!

The statistics are staggering. It is obvious that COBOL is neither dead nor quickly dying as many would suggest. On the contrary, COBOL is thriving. An important factor contributing to COBOL's popularity is its continuing evolution. Since its birth in 1960, there have been five major releases (see Table 1.1) plus an addendum. The next standard, ANSI-9X, will be number six. Each successive standard has provided new important features that result in improved programmer productivity.

Table 1-1: COBOL Release History

YEAR	CHARACTERISTICS
1960	Initial Release
1961	Added Identification Division
1965	Table handling added
1968	Seven modules were defined and standardized
1974	Improved table handling, random access, report writer, debug module, subprograms
1985	Structured programming constructs added plus DB2 and SQL support
1989	(ADDENDUM) 42 intrinsic functions added
199X	Object extensions plus dynamic table allocation, bit and boolean data types

COBOL admittedly has an image problem. Some see it as an old-fashioned, extremely verbose text-based development language limited to mainframe batch applications.

The truth is, COBOL is a dynamic, highly-productive development tool whose syntax is understood by literally millions of applications developers. The dynamic nature of the language is clearly demonstrated by its evolution. Vendors continue to develop and promote COBOL-based tools which compete favorably in today's development climate, including graphical interfaces and client-server architectures (Katz, et al., 1995). COBOL-9X is a logical continuation of this trend.

The Micro Focus Company

The Micro Focus company was founded in 1976 to provide programming tools for applications developers. Today it is an international firm with headquarters in Palo Alto, California and offices worldwide with over 600 employees. Micro Focus developed the first COBOL compiler for a microcomputer in 1977 and in 1981 produced the industry's first visual debugger: the Animator.

In 1995 Micro Focus introduced the first true 32-bit COBOL compiler that supported both procedural and object-oriented COBOL. In 1996 the firm released the first native Windows 95 development environment for COBOL: Visual Object COBOL.

Additional information can be found on the World Wide Web at the Micro Focus Home Page at http://WWW. MICROFOCUS.COM.

About Micro Focus Personal COBOL for Windows

The Micro Focus Personal COBOL for Windows system is a powerful tool designed to help you learn about COBOL, both procedural and object-oriented. The system supports several COBOL standards: ANSI -74, ANSI-85, and the anticipated ANSI-9X.

This system enables you to enter, compile, execute and debug a program quite rapidly. The system consists of several important tools:

- The Animator enables you to edit, compile, execute and debug programs
- The Browser lets you work with several programs at once
- Personal Dialog System (PDS) creates graphical user interfaces
- The Class Library contains numerous programs
- The Online Help System provides quick answers to questions
- The Run Time System (RTS) runs compiled code

The system runs with either Windows 3.1 or Windows 95 and is distributed on either a CD-ROM or diskettes.

Bibliography

Howard, K. "Explaining Object-Oriented Concepts to COBOL Programmers," <u>Object Magazine</u>, March-April 1993, 59-63.

Katz, P., Kornatowski, J., Loomis, M., Shukla, A., and O'Brien, L., "Debatable Data," <u>Computer Language</u>, 10 (1), January 1993, 55-62.

Lauer, J., and Graf, D., COBOL: Icon of the Past or Symbol of the Future? <u>Journal of Computer Information Systems</u>, 34(3), Spring 1994, 67-71.

Litecky, C., and Arnett, K., A Longitudinal Study of the Most Wanted Skills in the MIS Job Market, <u>1994 National Proceedings of the Decision Sciences Institute</u>, 873-875.

McFarland, D.E., COBOL Forges Ahead, <u>Computerworld</u>, June 5, 1995

Saade, H. and Wallace, A., COBOL-97: A Status Report, <u>Dr. Dobb's Journal</u>, 20 (10), October 1995, 52-54.

Snyder, J.R., <u>Encyclopedia of Computers</u>, Macmillan, Vol 1, 1992.

Chapter 2

Installing Micro Focus
Personal COBOL

System Requirements

Typographical Conventions

Windows 3.1 Installation

Windows 95 Installation

System Requirements

The Micro Focus Personal COBOL system is distributed either on diskettes or CD-ROM. To install and run Personal COBOL for Windows you will need a personal computer with the following *minimum* resources:

- A 386, 486, or Pentium processor

- Windows 3.1, Windows 95, or Windows NT

- 22 megabytes of available disk space

- 8 megabytes of memory (RAM)

- A VGA monitor

Typographical Conventions

The following typographical conventions are used in this manual:

- Menu Selections are **Boldface.** Example: **File**

- The vertical bar | is used to denote successive menu choices. For example, **File|New** means to click the **File** menu, and then click **New**.

- The plus symbol, **+** means to press two or more keys at the same time. For example Ctrl+B means to press the Ctrl key and the B key together.

- `Courier font` is used to denote COBOL source code. Example: `Compute`.

- *Italicized words* indicate important vocabulary. Example: *Hypertext*

- Items enclosed in quotes are to be entered exactly as shown. Do <u>not</u> key in the quotes. For example: Enter "MYFIRST.CBL"

Windows 3.1 Installation

To install Personal COBOL for Windows on a PC running Windows 3.1:
1. Insert the diskette named "Diskette 1 - setup" in the diskette drive or the CD-ROM in the CD Drive.

2. From the Program Manager window click **File|Run**.

3. In the Command Line box type "A:SETUP" for diskettes or "D:SETUP" for CD-ROM.
   Note: "A:" is the diskette drive letter and "D:" is the CD drive letter.
   If your drive has a different letter (such as B:) then enter that letter.

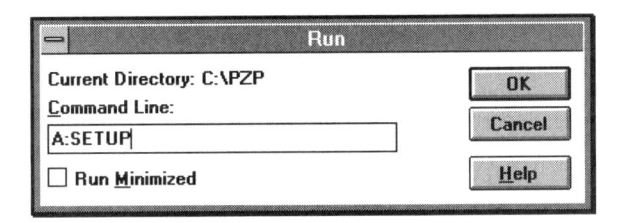

4. Click **OK** in the Run window.

5. Click **OK** in the Welcome window to continue the installation.

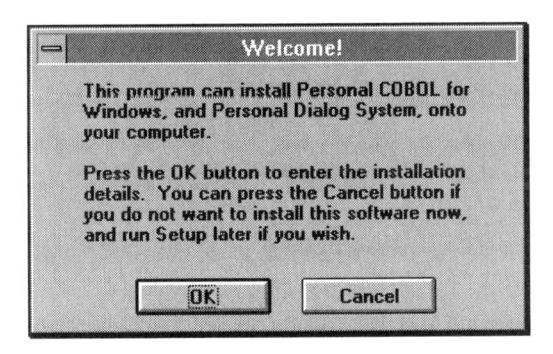

6. Enter your Name and Organization in the License & Registration window, and then click **OK**.

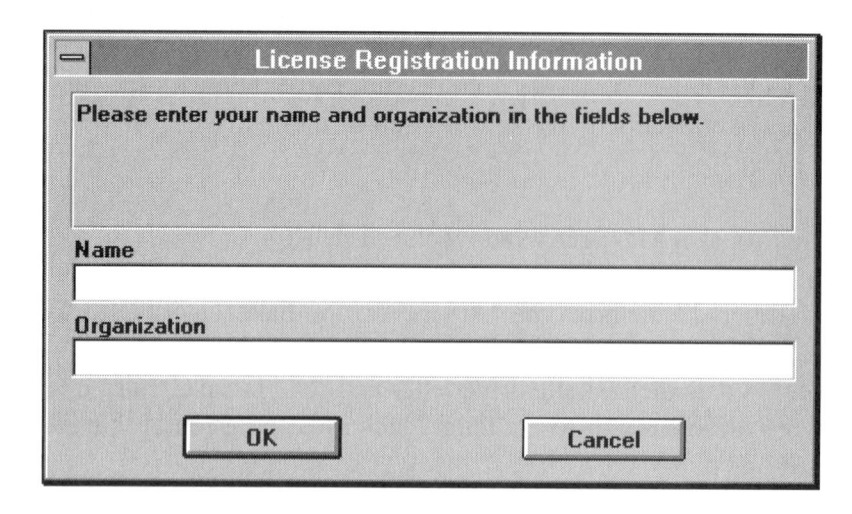

7. Click **YES** if your Name is correct; otherwise click **NO** and make corrections.

8. Normally you will want the system installed in the default directory named **\PCOBWIN.** To do this, click **OK** in the Choose Destination Directory window or, if you prefer, enter another directory name and then click **OK**.

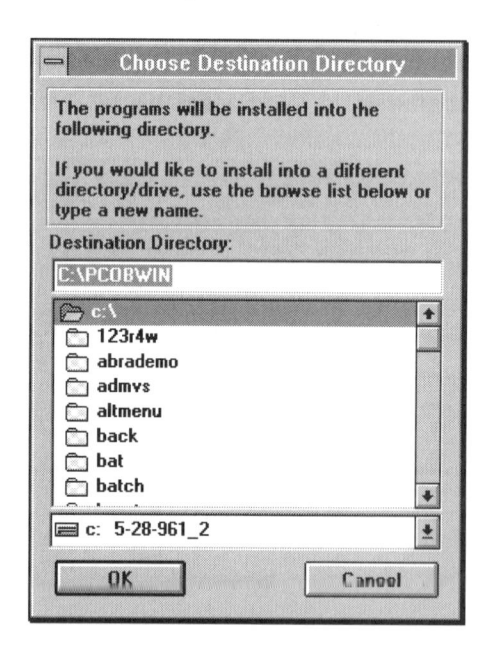

9. The COBOL Environment Settings window gives you three options: **Modify, Leave,** and **Abort**. Normally you will want to modify your AUTOEXEC.BAT and CONFIG.SYS files to automatically set the environment for Personal COBOL. Unless you have a clear reason for not wanting this feature, click **Modify**.

10. Click **OK** on the Select Program Manager Group Window. Or, if you wish, you can specify a different Group

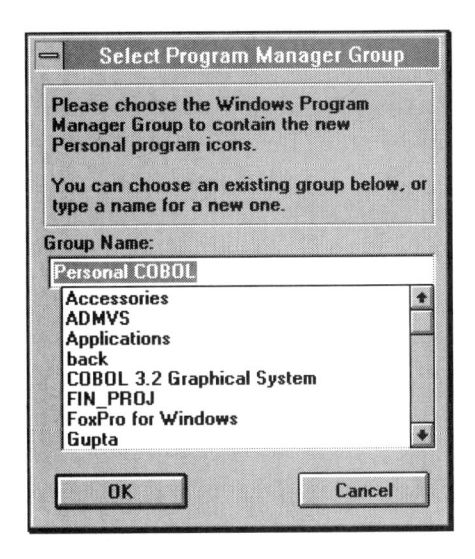

11. If your system came on diskette, insert the next diskette when prompted and click **OK**. Continue as prompted until all diskettes have been loaded.

12. When the Installation Process is complete, you will be asked if you wish to read the "ReadMe" file. Click **OK**.

13. The ReadMe file contains additional documentation. You can browse through this information as you wish. In addition, there is a **ReadMe** selection in the Personal COBOL Program group you can select later. Close the ReadMe window when you are ready to proceed.

14. Your Personal COBOL Program Group window will appear:

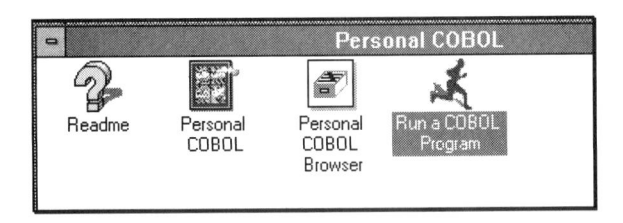

15. You may get a final window indicating you need to reboot. Click OK. This window simply tells you that you need to restart your computer before the environment variables for Personal COBOL will be activated.

16. You are now ready to begin using Personal COBOL for Windows.

Windows 95 Installation

To install Personal COBOL for Windows on a PC running Windows 95:

1. If your system came on diskettes, insert the diskette named "Diskette 1 - setup" in the diskette drive. If your system came on CD-ROM, insert the CD in the CD drive.

2. Click the Start button.

3. Click **Settings**.

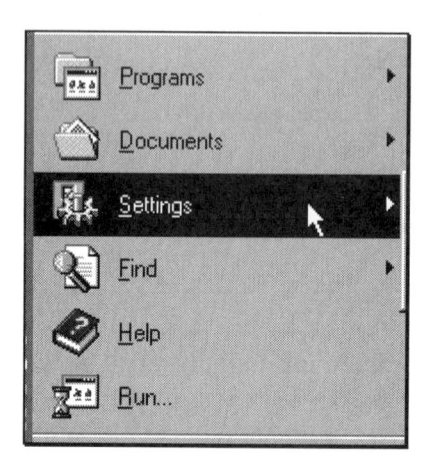

4. Click **Control Panel**.

5. Double click **Add/Remove Programs**.

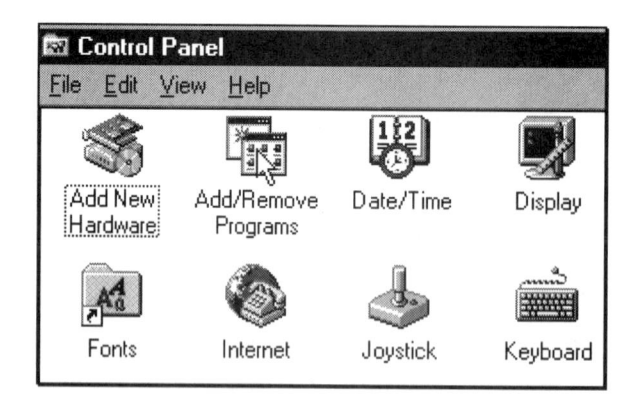

6. Click **Install** in the Add/Remove Programs Properties window.

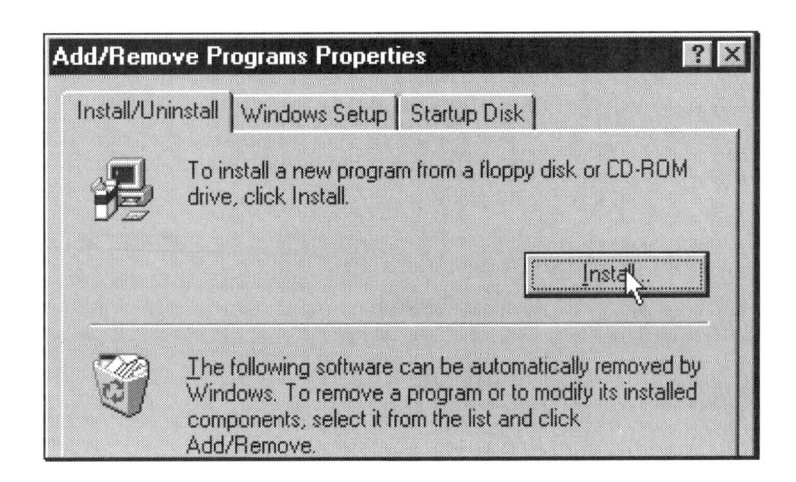

7. Click **Next** in the Install Program From Floppy or CD-ROM window.

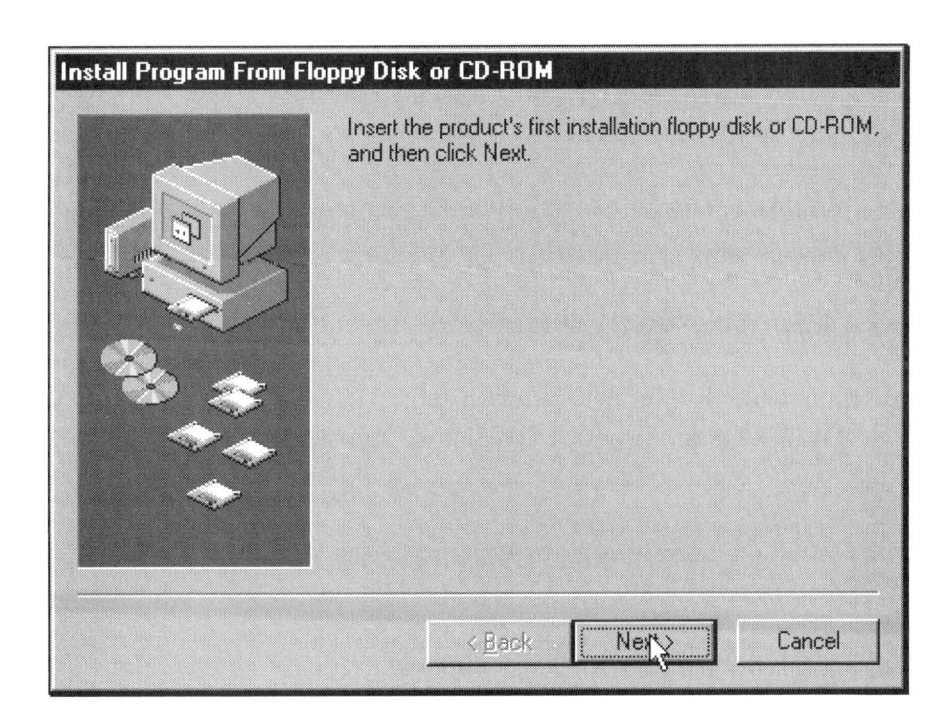

8. Windows should locate the "SETUP.EXE" file and display it in the command line. If not, key in "A:SETUP.EXE" for diskettes or "D:SETUP.EXE" for CD-ROM. Click **Finish**.

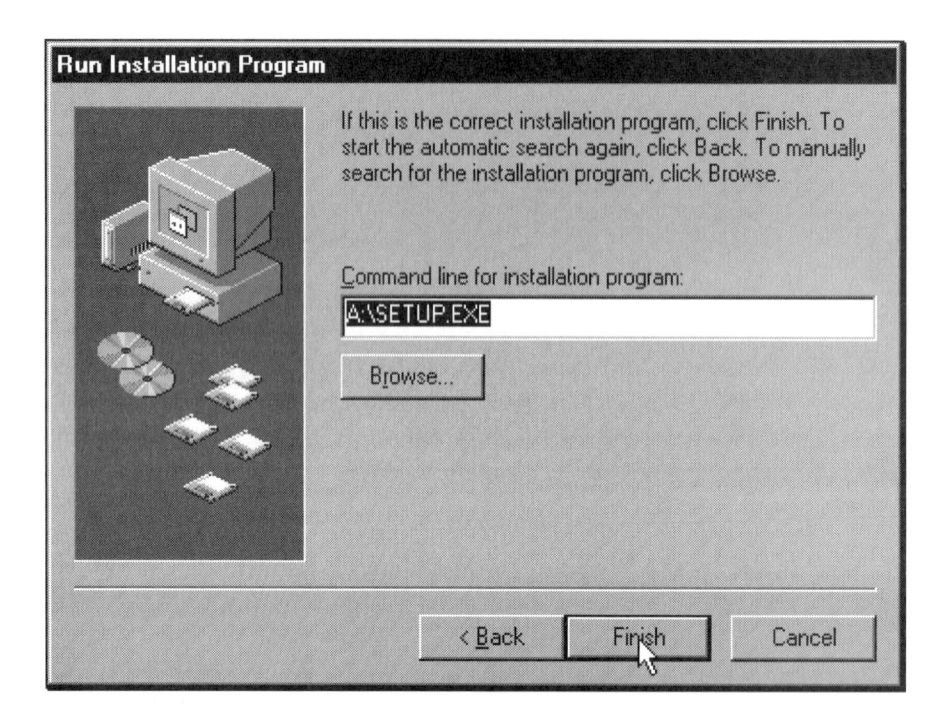

9. Click **OK** in the Welcome window.

10. Enter your Name and Organization in the License & Registration window, then Click **OK**.

11. Click **YES** if your Name is correct; otherwise click **NO** and make corrections.

12. Normally, you will want the System installed in the default directory named **\PCOBWIN**. To do this, click **OK** in the Choose Destination Directory window or, if you prefer, enter another directory name and then click **OK**.

13. Click **OK** on the Select Program Manager Group window. Or, if you wish, you can specify a different Group.

14. The COBOL Environment Settings window gives you three options: **Modify**, **Leave**, and **Abort**. Normally you will want to modify your AUTOEXEC.BAT and CONFIG.SYS files to automatically set the environment for Personal COBOL. Unless you have a clear reason for not wanting this feature, click **Modify**.

15. If your system came on diskettes, insert the next diskette when prompted and click **OK**. Continue as prompted until all diskettes have been loaded.

16. When the installation process is complete, you will be asked if you wish to read the "ReadMe" file. Click **OK**.

17. The ReadMe file contains additional documentation. You can browse through this information as you wish. In addition, there is a **ReadMe** selection in the Personal COBOL Program group you can select later. Close the ReadMe window when you are ready to proceed.

18. You may get a final window named Reboot Next. Click OK. This window simply tells you that you need to restart your computer before the environment variables for Personal COBOL will be activated. This is a good time to click the **Start** icon, and then click **Shut Down**. In the Shut Down Windows window, select **Restart the Computer**. Your system will then reset and restart.

19. You are now ready to begin using Personal COBOL for Windows.

Chapter 3

Exploring
Micro Focus
Personal COBOL

Using Online Help Resources

Using The Animator

Using The Browser

This chapter introduces you to the On-line Help system, the Animator, and the Browser. A small procedural (non object-oriented) COBOL program will be executed to illustrate the use of both the Animator and Browser.

The following typographical conventions are used:
- Menu Selections are **Boldface.** Example: **File**
- The vertical bar | is used to denote successive menu choices. For example, **File|New** means to click the **File** menu, and then click **New**.
- The plus symbol, **+** means to press two or more keys at the same time. For example Ctrl+B means to press the Ctrl key and the B key together.
- `Courier font` is used to denote COBOL source code. Example: `Compute`.
- *Italicized words* indicate important vocabulary. Example: *Hypertext*
- Items enclosed in quotes are to be entered exactly as shown. Do <u>not</u> key in the quotes. For example: Enter "MYFIRST.CBL"

Using On-line Help

To Access On-line Help:

1. Launch the Animator. You will see the screen shown in Figure 3.1.
   - If you have Windows 3.1, double click the Animator icon in the Personal COBOL Program Group window.
   - If you have Windows 95, click the Start button, point to Programs, point to Personal COBOL, and then click the Animator icon.

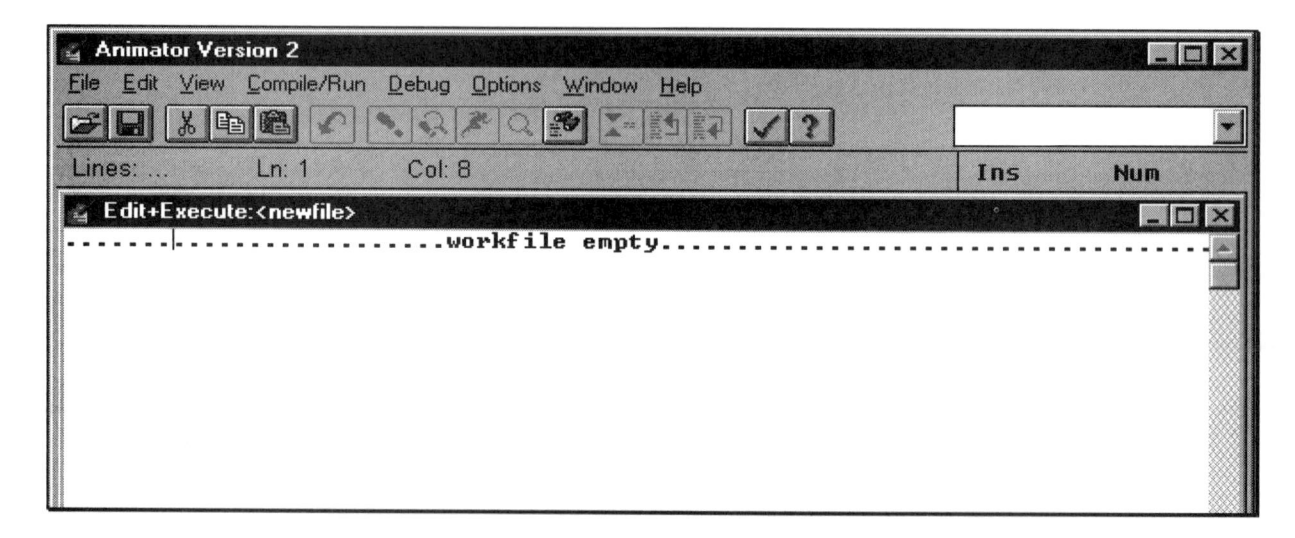

Figure 3.1: The Animator Window

2. Point to the Help menu and click the left mouse button to see the drop-down menu.

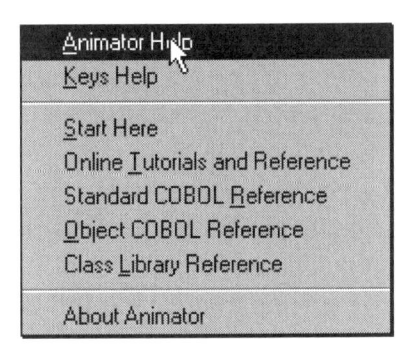

Figure 3.2: The Animator Help Menu

3. Click Animator Help. This selection opens the window shown in Figure 3.3. The help facilities in the Personal COBOL system employs *hypertext links*. Clicking one of these links will display a window of related information. These links are underlined and displayed in a contrasting color. When you move the cursor to a word that is a *hyperlink*, the cursor changes shape from an arrow to a hand. Figure 3.3 points to "Getting Started With Animator" and the arrow is now displayed as a hand with the index finger pointing to the *hyperlink*.

Using Personal COBOL Animator

Animator – also known as Animator V2 – is a full function tool for creating, modifying, testing and debugging your code. It is a powerful and highly configurable editor, debugger and compiler all rolled into one. This on-line help describes Animator V2's features.

NOTE: this help file is for all versions of Micro Focus Animator V2 and includes some features which are available only in the professional versions of Micro Focus Animator V2. A few features described here are not available in Personal COBOL.

Getting Started

Getting Started with Animator
Hints & tips
Migrating from the Micro Focus COBOL Editor

Procedures

Debugging programs
Editing programs

Figure 3.3: Animator Help Window

4. Click "<u>Getting Started With Animator</u>" to display the screen in Figure 3.4. Notice that it too has several *hyperlinks*. This example points to "<u>Editing Your Program.</u>" These links give you navigation ability to explore topics until you get the information you want. At the top of each help screen, beneath the menu bar, there are additional navigation tools. **Contents** displays the help topics in *hyperlink* format. **Search** displays a window which gives you the option to find a particular topic. The **Back** button, as the name suggests, returns to the previous help screen, and **Print** will display a Print dialog window that enables you to print the help information you are viewing. The **Index** button is similar to the **Contents** button, but it displays the Help Index in *hyperlink* form.

Getting Started

Animator V2 provides a complete development environment which you can use to create, analyze and optimize your source code.

This topic looks at the typical tasks and functions that you would use to create and test a program using Animator V2, and is especially useful if you are new to using Animator V2. These tasks and functions are listed below, in the usual order in which they would be performed:

1. Edit your program
2. Correct any editing mistakes
3. Correct syntax errors
4. Animate your program
5. Navigate through your program

See Also:

<u>Editing Your Program</u>
<u>Correcting Any Editing Mistakes</u>
<u>Correcting Syntax Errors</u>
<u>Animating Your Program</u>
<u>Navigating Through Your Program</u>
<u>Using Animator V2</u>

Figure 3.4: Getting Started With Animator Window

5. Now is a good time to explore Help on your own. Navigate through several windows to see what you can find. Incidentally, you can also activate the online help by pressing F1.

6. Click **File|Exit** when you are finished.

Using The Animator

If you have not already done so, launch the Animator. You will see the screen shown in Figure 3.5.

- If you have Windows 3.1, double click the Animator icon in the Personal COBOL Program Group window.
- If you have Windows 95, click the Start button, point to Programs, point to Personal COBOL, and then click the Animator icon.

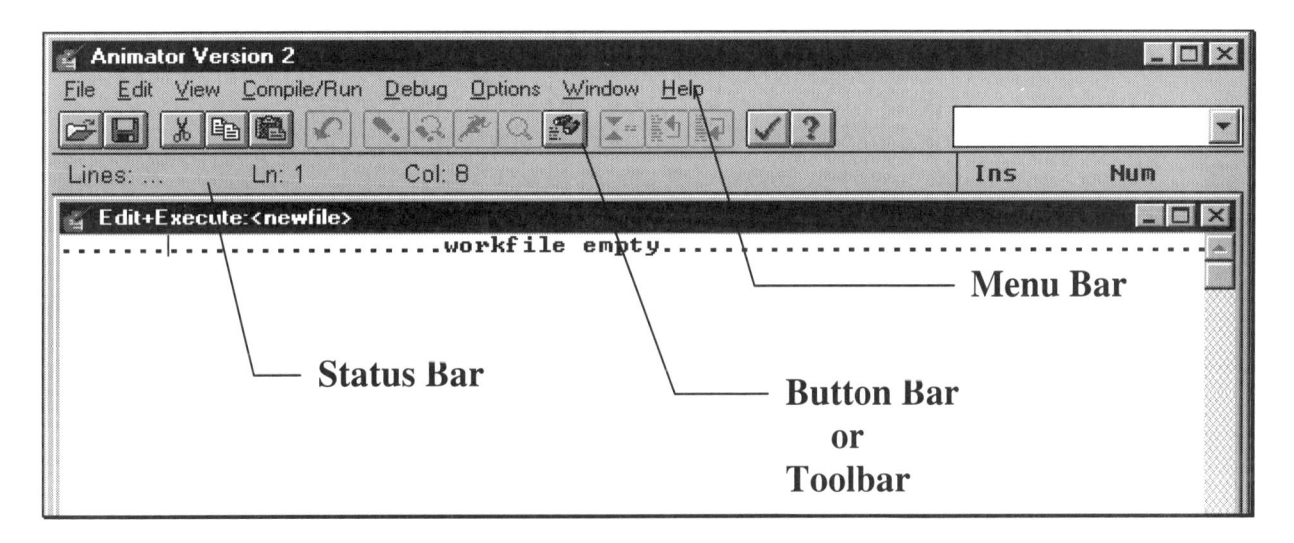

Figure 3.5: The Animator Edit Screen

The Animator is used to edit a COBOL program. You can use the Animator to write a new program or to make changes to one already written. However, the Animator is much more than an editor. You can compile and execute a program using the Animator. You can also step through the execution of a program and display the contents of fields in a program. These techniques are illustrated in Chapter 4.

To become acquainted with the Animator window, look at the top part of Figure 3.5. This window has the familiar menu bar which is used to activate pull-down menus. Right below the menu bar there is a button bar or toolbar which displays icons to quickly activate the common menu commands such as open a file and save a file. Although the icons usually clearly suggest their function, a descriptive message is displayed at the bottom of the screen as you point to them. Below the toolbar there is a status bar which will be used shortly.

Using the Editor in Animator:

The Editor in the Animator behaves similar to a word processor. You may enter, change and delete text. To enter text, simply type it in. You can select or *mark* text by pointing to the first character in the text, pressing the left mouse button, and dragging the mouse across the text. You may mark one character, a word, a line, or multiple lines using this technique. The following keys can speed your editing. Click **Help|Keys Help** for a complete listing of the keys and their uses.

Key	Action to Be Taken
Alt+BkSp	undo the last action (you can also click **Edit|Undo**)
Alt+Shift +BkSp	redo the last action (you can also click **Edit|Redo**)
BkSp	deletes the previous character
Ctrl+Ins	copy the marked text (you can also click **Edit|Copy**)
Del	deletes the following character or marked text
Enter	goes to a new line
F3	inserts a line
F4	deletes a line (you can also click **Edit|Delete Line**)
F5	repeats a line (you can also click **Edit|Repeat Line**)
F6	restores a line previously deleted (you can also click **Edit|Restore Line**)
Ins	toggles between insert and overstrike mode
Shift+Del	cut the marked text (you can also click **Edit|Cut**)
Shift+Ins	paste (you can also click **Edit|Paste**)
Shift+Tab	tabs 4 positions at a time to the left
Tab	tabs 4 positions at a time to the right

To Enter a New COBOL Program:

1. Click **File** in the menu bar.

2. Click **New**. In other words, click **File|New**.
   Notice that the status bar shows your cursor located at Line 1 and Column 8. This bar also tells you whether you have Insert (Ins), CapsLock (Caps) or NumLock (Num) toggled.

3. In the edit pane key in

```
Identification Division.
```

and then press return. Here the first letter of each word is capitalized, but the case is unimportant. You can use all upper case or all lower case if you wish.

4. Key in the rest of the program as shown in Figure 3.6.

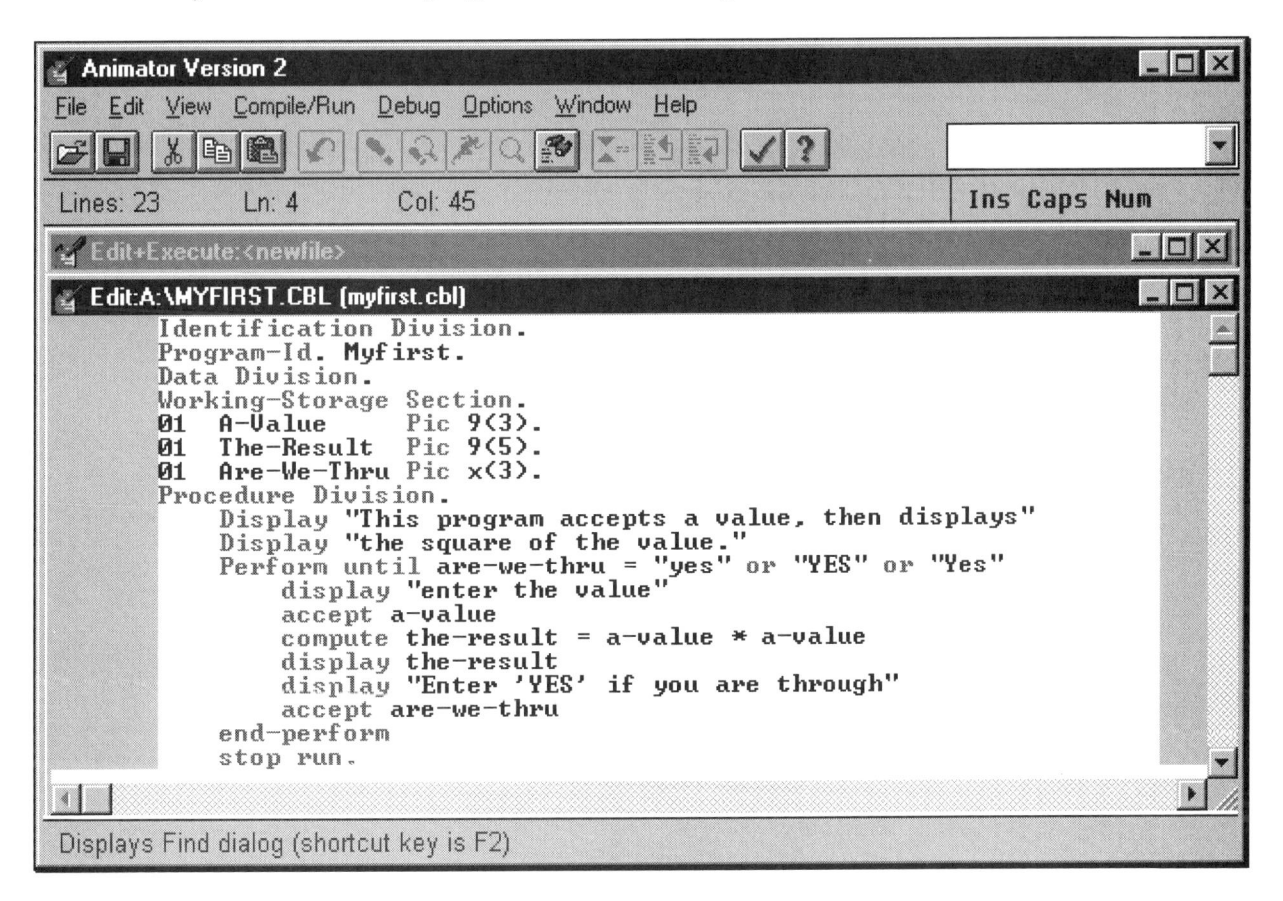

Figure 3.6: MYFIRST COBOL Program

You can see that the Animator uses different colors for different parts of the program. The Animator uses these different colors to let you quickly see the various components of a program. The default colors are red for data names and green for COBOL verbs and reserved words. You can customize these colors if you wish. Click **Options|Color...** to make your color choices.

To Compile a COBOL Program:

Next let's compile the program, or to use a term commonly used in the Personal COBOL environment, *check* the program. Checking a COBOL program does two things: first, the program is scanned to identify any syntax errors; second, if no serious syntax errors are found, the compiler produces an *intermediate* file. This file has a suffix or extension of "INT" and can be executed using Personal COBOL's Run-time system.

1. Click either the check button in the toolbar ☑ or click **Compile/Run|Compile Program**.

2. The Animator will then display a Save As window. Enter the file name "MYFIRST.CBL" to save the program. The Animator then checks for syntax errors and compiles the program.

3. If you made any typing mistakes, you will need to correct them; then recheck the program. If you have errors, you will first see a window similar to the following.

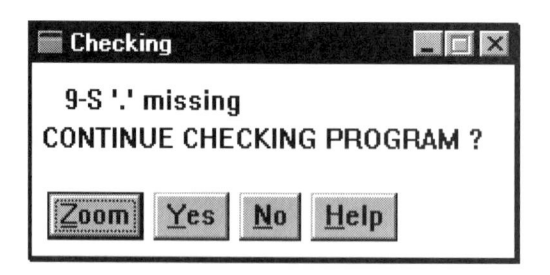

Click the Zoom button to continue checking. You will then see a Complete with errors message.

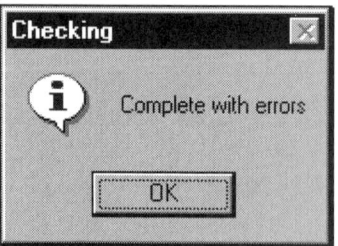

Click **OK**. The lines containing errors will be highlighted for you. Compare your program to Figure 3.6 to locate typing errors. Correct any errors and recheck the program.

To Execute a COBOL Program:

The Animator actually has two operating modes: *Edit* mode and *Execution* mode. As the name suggests, Edit mode is used for editing and checking programs only. Execution mode is used for editing, checking <u>and executing</u> programs. The mode is specified in the upper left part of the text window shown in Figure 3.6. The important thing for you to know is that you cannot execute a program from a window that is in Edit Mode. To resolve this, we click **File|Open for execution** and enter "MYFIRST.INT". The *INT* file is the executable intermediate program file created by the compiler.

Notice that when you open a file for execution, the heading in the text window changes from "Edit" to "Edit + Execute" , and several more icons in the toolbar become available.

    1. Click **Compile/Run|Run**.

    2. Enter "3" when prompted.

    3. Enter "Yes" when prompted. Figure 3.7 shows the execution of MYFIRST.

```
 Animator V2 Text Window
This program accepts a value, then displays
the square of the value.
enter the value
3
00009
Enter 'YES' if you are through
YES_
```

Figure 3.7: The Execution of MYFIRST Program

    4. Click **OK** when you see the Stop Run message.

    5. Click **File|Exit** to exit the Animator.

Using The Browser

1. Launch the Browser. You will see the screen shown in Figure 3.8.
   - If you have Windows 3.1, double click the Browser icon in the Personal COBOL Program Group window.
   - If you have Windows 95, click the Start button, point to Programs, point to Personal COBOL, and then click the Browser icon.

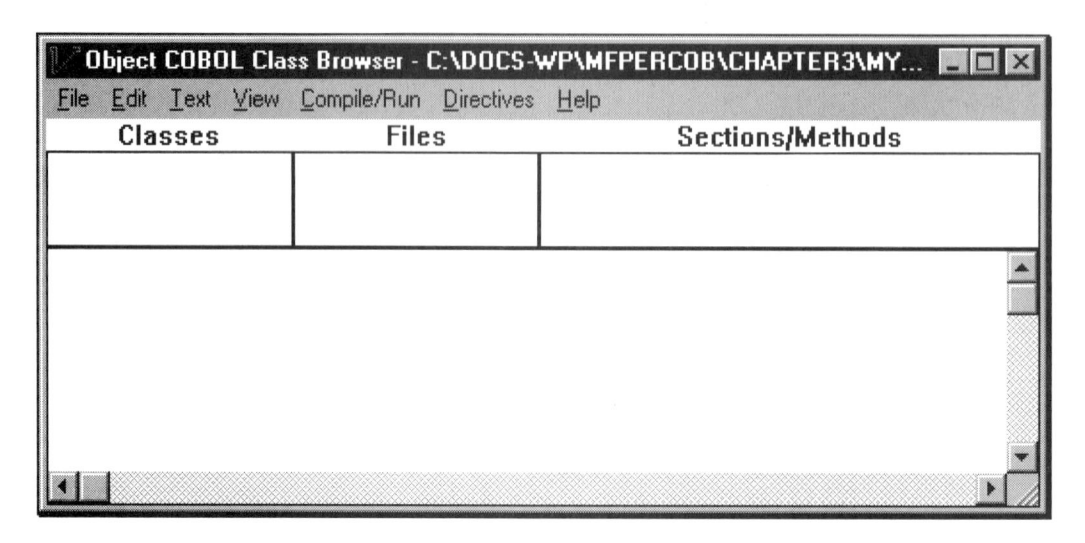

Figure 3.8: The Browser Window

Although the Browser window has a completely different appearance, you can do many of the same things from this window that you do from the Animator. In fact, you can launch the Animator from The Browser. The two work closely together. The primary difference between the Browser and the Animator is that the Browser is designed to work with several programs at once while the Animator works with one program at a time. Working with several programs as once is especially important when writing Object COBOL class programs, which you will do in Chapter 5.

The Browser requires us to specify a *Project,* which is simply a collection of programs. In the simple example here, there will be only one program in the project. In Chapter 5 there will be a project with two programs.

2. Click **File|Open/New Project**.

3. Enter "MYFIRST.PRJ" in the File Name window.
   Notice that this project name appears in the top part of the Browser window. Also, notice this window has a menu bar similar to that found in the Animator. The rest of the Browser window looks a lot different! This window has four panes. The three small ones across the top are Classes, Files, and Sections/Methods. The large pane in the bottom half of the window is used for editing the program.

4. Click **File|Open** and enter "MYFIRSTCBL", and then click **OK.** You should now have the window shown in Figure 3.9.

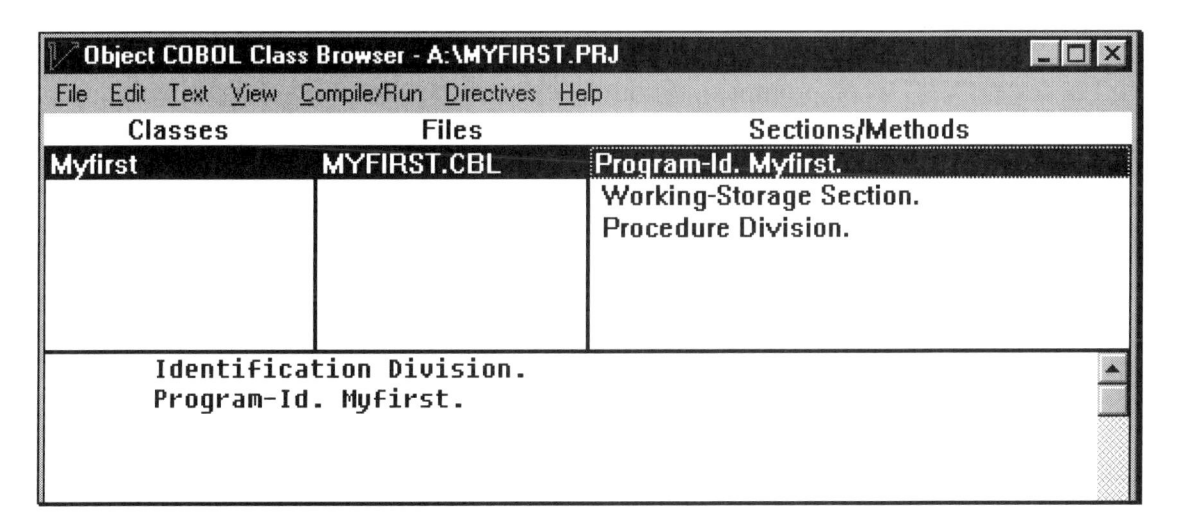

Figure 3.9: MYFIRST Program in the Browser Window

5. In the Sections/Methods pane, click Program-Id, Working-Storage, and Procedure Division one at a time. Notice that the text editing pane displays the contents of whichever division or section you have highlighted in the Sections/Methods pane. Although at first this may seem a little strange, it will quickly become an important tool for viewing the various parts of a COBOL program quickly.

6. Click **Compile/Run** in the menu bar to display the pull-down menu.

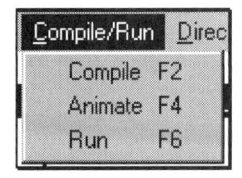

From this menu you can Compile, Animate or Run a program. Notice you can either click on the Menu choices or use function keys.

7. Click **Compile** or press F2.

8. Click **OK** when compilation is finished.

9. Click **Animate** or press F4. You should now see the somewhat familiar Animator window that you explored earlier in this chapter.

10. Click **Compile/Run|Run** to execute the program.

11. Enter "3" when prompted.

12. Enter "Yes" when prompted. Figure 3.7 shows the execution of MYFIRST.

13. Click **OK** when you see the Stop Run message.

14. Click **File|Exit** to exit the Animator.

15. Click **File|Exit** to exit the Browser.

Chapter 4

Developing Programs Using The Animator

Entering and Editing a Program

This chapter continues with the exploration of the Animator. You will begin by entering another small COBOL program named "MYSECOND." You may wish to review the section on Typographical Conventions and Using The Editor in Chapter 3 if you have not done so.

To reduce the amount of typing, the division and section headers in MYSECOND have been omitted, and are not required by the ANSI 199X standard. The purpose of MYSECOND is to compute the present value of a dollar amount to be received in the future. A dollar today is worth more than a dollar to be received in the future. Today's value, the present value, is determined by the interest rate and the number of years until the amount is received. The formula is

```
COMPUTE Present-Value =
    Future-Value / (1 + Interest-Rate) ** Number-Of-Years
```

The "**" symbol means "raise to the power of." The intrinsic function *Present-Value* could be used instead of the formula.

To Enter MYSECOND Program:

1. If you have not already done so, launch the Animator and then enter the program as shown in Figure 4.1 below. The program contains two *intentional* errors, so enter it *exactly* as shown.

```
Edit:C:\PCOBWIN\GETSTART\MYSECOND.CBL (mysecond.cbl*)
 1 Program-Id. MYSECOND.
 2 01   Future-Value    Pic 9(5).
 3 01   Interest-Rate   Pic V99999.
 4 01   Number-Of-Years Pic 9(3).
 5 01   Present-Value   Pic Z,ZZ9.99.
   01   Are-We-Through  Pic X(3).
 7      88 We-Are-Thru    Values "YES" "Yes" "yes".
 8 Procedure Division.
 9      Display "This program computes Present Value"
10      Perform until We-Are-Thru
11          Display "Enter the Future Value (whole dollar amount)"
12          Accept Future-Value
13          Display "Enter the Interest Rate (.nnnnn)"
14          Accept Interest-Rate
15          Display "Enter the Number of Years in the future"
16          Accept Number-of-Years
17          Compute Present-Value Rounded =
18              Future-Value  (1 + Interest-Rate) ** Number-Of-Years
19          Display "The Present Value is: ", Present-Value
20          Display "Enter 'YES' to Stop, any key to continue"
21          Accept Are-We-Thru
22      End-Perform
23      Stop Run.
```

Figure 4.1: MYSECOND Program

2. Next, compile the program by clicking the Check button 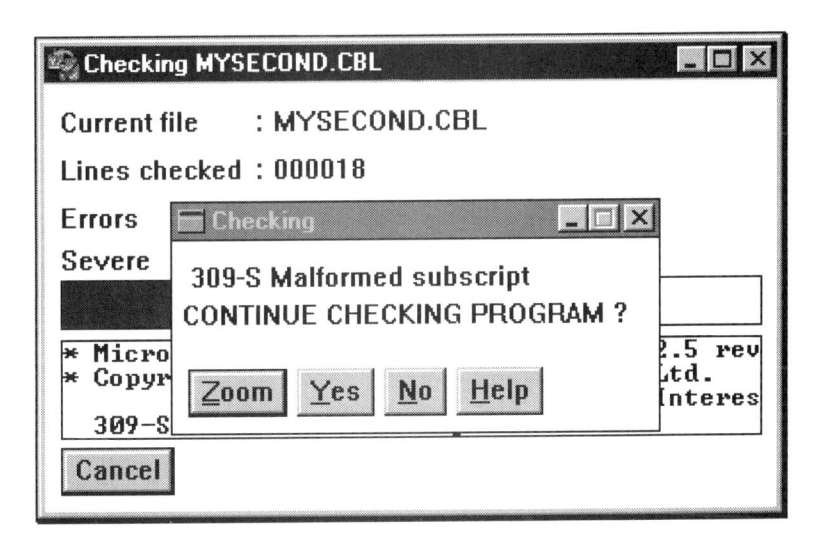, or click **Compile/Run|Compile Program**. You should get a window similar to Figure 4.2, telling you an error has been detected.

Figure 4.2: Compiler Errors in MYSECOND Program

3. Click the Yes button to continue checking the program.

4. You will see a second window telling you that ARE-WE-THRU is not declared . Click Yes to continue.

5. When the compiler has finished you will see the window shown in Figure 4.3. Click the OK button.

Figure 4.3: Complete With Errors Window

At this point you should be looking at a screen similar to Figure 4.4. There should be two errors in the program, and these are highlighted in the Animator window. One of these errors occurred because we spelled the field named "ARE-WE-THROUGH" as "ARE-WE-THRU" in the Procedure Division. The other error is because we omitted the division symbol "/" in the COMPUTE statement.

```
Edit:C:\PCOBWIN\GETSTART\MYSECOND.CBL (mysecond.cbl)         _ □ ☒
    1  Program-Id. MYSECOND.
    2  01   Future-Value    Pic 9(5).
    3  01   Interest-Rate   Pic U99999.              |
    4  01   Number-Of-Years Pic 9(3).
    5  01   Present-Value   Pic Z,ZZ9.99.
    6  01   Are-We-Through  Pic X(3).
    7       88 We-Are-Thru     Values "YES" "Yes" "yes".
    8  Procedure Division.
    9       Display "This program computes Present Value"
   10       Perform until We-Are-Thru
   11           Display "Enter the Future Value (whole dollar amount)"
   12           Accept Future-Value
   13           Display "Enter the Interest Rate (.nnnnn)"
   14           Accept Interest-Rate
   15           Display "Enter the Number of Years in the future"
   16           Accept Number-of-Years
   17           Compute Present-Value Rounded =
Error>             Future-Value  (1 + Interest-Rate) ** Number-Of-Year
   19           Display "The Present Value is: ", Present-Value
   20           Display "Enter 'YES' to Stop, any key to continue"
Error>         Accept Are-We-Thru
   22       End-Perform
   23       Stop Run.
```

Figure 4.4: MYSECOND Program With Errors Highlighted

You should also have the Syntax Errors window shown in Figure 4.5. This window lists all of the syntax errors the compiler has detected. You can double click on the error in this window to position the cursor to the line in the source program that contains the error. You can also click **Help|Standard COBOL Reference** then click **Syntax Errors** to locate a more detailed explanation of the error. Use the error number (such as 309) as a reference.

```
Syntax Errors: c:\pcobwin\getstart\mysecond.msg
 309-S Malformed subscript
   12-S Operand ARE-WE-THRU is not declared
```

Figure 4.5: Syntax Errors window

Let's go ahead and correct these errors. One of the (many) nice things about the Animator is how easy it is to make changes in a program.

To Correct The Syntax Errors:

1. To correct the "ARE-WE-THRU" error simply move the cursor to the "ARE-WE-THROUGH" name at line 6 and change it to "ARE-WE-THRU."

2. Insert an "/" in the compute statement which should now appear as:

```
COMPUTE Present-Value Rounded =
    Future-Value / (1 + Interest-Rate) ** Number-Of-Years
```

3. Click **File|Save** to save the corrected program.

4. Re-check the program. You should now have an error-free program which is ready to execute. The program should appear as shown in Figure 4.6.

```
Edit:C:\PCOBWIN\GETSTART\MYSECOND.CBL (mysecond.cbl)            _ □
 1 Program-Id. MYSECOND.
 2 01   Future-Value    Pic 9(5).
 3 01   Interest-Rate   Pic U99999.
 4 01   Number-Of-Years Pic 9(3).
 5 01   Present-Value   Pic Z,ZZ9.99.
 6 01   Are-We-Thru     Pic X(3).
 7      88 We-Are-Thru    Values "YES" "Yes" "yes".
 8 Procedure Division.
 9     Display "This program computes Present Value"
10     Perform until We-Are-Thru
11         Display "Enter the Future Value (whole dollar amount)"
12         Accept Future-Value
13         Display "Enter the Interest Rate (.nnnnn)"
14         Accept Interest-Rate
15         Display "Enter the Number of Years in the future"
16         Accept Number-of-Years
17         Compute Present-Value Rounded =
18             Future-Value / (1 + Interest-Rate) ** Number-Of-Years
19         Display "The Present Value is: ", Present-Value
20         Display "Enter 'YES' to Stop, any key to continue"
21         Accept Are-We-Thru
22     End-Perform
23     Stop Run.
```

Figure 4.6: Error-free MYSECOND Program

Now that we have an error-free program, let's run it. The Animator can execute a program in one of two *modes*: *Run Mode* or *Step Mode*. In Run mode, the program executes normally. However, in Step mode the program executes *one statement at a time*. It steps through the program execution. We also have the option, as demonstrated later, of running the program up to a specific statement, and then changing modes. Each mode is discussed separately in the following paragraphs.

Run Mode

When we execute a program in Run Mode, we are executing the program normally. That is, one statement is executed, then the next, without intervention, unless of course we have an error.

To Execute MYSECOND In Run Mode:

1. Open MYSECOND for execution by clicking **File|Open for execution...** and key in "MYSECOND." This should load the intermediate file, "MYSECOND.INT" created earlier when you checked the program.

2. To begin running the program in Run Mode, either click the Run button 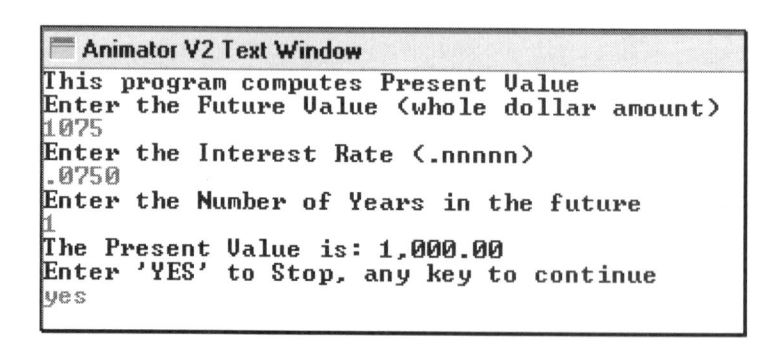, or click **Compile/Run|Run**.

3. The program should display the message to enter a Future Value.
   Enter "1075." (Don't type the quotes).

4. The program next asks for an Interest Rate. Enter ".0750."

5. Next, the program asks for the Number of Years. Enter "1." The program should then display "1,000.00."

6. Enter "YES" at the "are you through" question. Your output screen should appear similar to Figure 4.7 below.

```
Animator V2 Text Window
This program computes Present Value
Enter the Future Value (whole dollar amount)
1075
Enter the Interest Rate (.nnnnn)
.0750
Enter the Number of Years in the future
1
The Present Value is: 1,000.00
Enter 'YES' to Stop, any key to continue
yes
```

Figure 4.7: MYSECOND Output Screen

7. Click OK when you get the Stop Run Message.

8. If you wish, you may rerun the program by clicking **Compile/Run|Restart Application**, then clicking the Run button.

Step Mode

Next, we will execute the program using Step Mode.

To Execute MYSECOND In Step Mode:

1. First, click **Compile/Run|Restart Application** to reset the system so we can run the program again.

2. To begin executing the program one statement at a time, click either the Step button [icon], or click **Compile/Run|Step**. The Display statement at line 10 should be highlighted.

3. Once you are in Step Mode, you can execute the next statement by either clicking the Step button, or pressing Ctrl+S. Execute through the Accept statement at line 12.

4. You should now see the text window. Enter values for Future Value, Interest Rate, and Number of Years.

5. When you are through, enter "YES" at the "are you through" question.

Setting Breakpoints

A *Breakpoint* is a marker you place in your program to temporarily pause the program execution. Once the statement with the Breakpoint is reached, program execution is suspended until you take some action. Usually, you will set a breakpoint so you can look more closely at code and data used by your program. You may set multiple breakpoints in a program.

To set a breakpoint you will click on the statement (to highlight it) where you want the Breakpoint placed, and then click **Debug|Set Breakpoint**. You can also set a Breakpoint by first highlighting the statement, then pressing Ctrl+B. And, you can simply double click on the statement to set a Breakpoint.

You can clear a Breakpoint by highlighting the statement, then click **Debug|Unset Breakpoint**, or simply double click the statement with the Breakpoint. You can also clear all Breakpoints by clicking **Debug|Clear all Breakpoints**.

4-8

To Execute MYSECOND With a Breakpoint:

1. Restart the application (**Compile/Run|Restart Application).**

2. Set a Breakpoint on the Compute statement at line 17. Your screen should now look like Figure 4.8.

```
Edit+Execute:C:\DOCS-WP\MFPERCOB\CHAPTER4\MYSECOND.INT (mysecond.cbl)
    7        88 We-Are-Thru    Values "YES" "Yes" "yes".
    8  Procedure Division.
    9        Display "This program computes Present Value"
   10        Perform until We-Are-Thru
   11            Display "Enter the Future Value (whole dollar amount)"
   12            Accept Future-Value
   13            Display "Enter the Interest Rate (.nnnnn)"
   14            Accept Interest-Rate
   15            Display "Enter the Number of Years in the future"
   16            Accept Number-of-Years
BrkPt>            Compute Present-Value Rounded =
   18                Future-Value / (1 + Interest-Rate) ** Number-Of-Years
   19            Display "The Present Value is: ", Present-Value
   20            Display "Enter 'YES' to Stop, any key to continue"
   21            Accept Are-We-Thru
   22        End-Perform
   23        Stop Run.
   24
```

Figure 4.8: MYSECOND Program with a Breakpoint

3. With the Breakpoint set on the Compute statement, execute the program in Run Mode. Click on either the Run button or click **Compile/Run|Run**.

4. Enter the values when prompted.

5. You should then get the message:

Figure 4.9: Breakpoint Encountered Message

6. Click OK, and you will see the program has stopped at the Compute statement.

7. Click the Run button and then enter "YES" when prompted to terminate the program.

Examining Data

Personal COBOL provides tools to look at data as a program executes. This feature is especially useful when debugging.

To Execute MYSECOND and Examine Data:

1. If you have not already done so, open MYSECOND program again for execution.

2. Double click on the Compute statement to set a Breakpoint.

3. Click the Run button to execute the program.

4. When prompted, enter "1075" Future Value, ".075" Interest Rate, and "1" Number of Years.

5. When you get to the Breakpoint encountered message, the screen should now look like Figure 4.9 in the previous section.

6. To look at the contents of the Present-Value field, click **Debug|Examine Data**, then enter "Present-Value" and click OK.

Figure 4.10: Examining Data

7. Next, click Monitor. You have instructed the system to monitor (display) the contents of Present-Value as the program executes. As you can see, Present-Value currently is empty.

8. Click the Step button . Watch the contents of Present-Value change to "1,000.00" as shown in Figure 4.11 when the compute statement is executed.

Figure 4.11: Contents of Present-Value After Compute

9. Enter "Yes" to stop the program, click OK at the Stop Run message, and close the Animator.

Printing a Program Listing

If you would like to have a printed listing of your program, click **File|Print**. This will display the Print window so you can specify the printer and format you wish to have.

Chapter 5

The World
of Object COBOL

Object-Oriented Concepts

Writing A Class Program

To Learn More

5-2

This chapter gives you an introduction to Object-oriented (OO) programming using Object COBOL. As outlined in Chapter 1, the next ANSI COBOL standard, ANSI-9X, will include object programming language extensions. The Personal COBOL for Windows system includes these extensions as they are currently defined. This means you can learn about OO programming and Object COBOL now.

The chapter first presents some basic OO concepts, and then describes Object COBOL and shows you how to execute a small Object COBOL program.

Object-Oriented Concepts

This section is a *summary* of OO concepts. At the end of this chapter are several references if you want to learn more. This brief section is not intended to be a thorough detailed discussion of OO. It is intended to help you get started.

As you study OO development, you will see some things that are very similar to traditional systems development, and you will see some things that are significantly different.

In the world of OO, we focus on things called *objects* and the interaction between these objects. In fact, many objects are really **nouns**. Recall that a noun is a *person*, *place*, or *thing*. A thing can be tangible or it can be intangible. An object can therefore be a person, such as a customer or a student , a place like department, a tangible thing such as such as an airplane or book, or an intangible thing like a reservation or transaction.

In an OO system, we write software to model these objects and their interactions. Because OO systems deal with objects and their interactions, these systems often resemble a simulation of real-world activities. A **customer** makes a **reservation**; a **student** enrolls in a **course**.

Objects need to "know things" and need to be able to "do things." For example, a Student object needs to **know** its name and identification number. In addition, a Student object must be able to **tell** us its name and identification number.

Software objects, which model the real-world objects, likewise "know things" and can "do things." In OO terminology, the things the object knows are called *Attributes* and the things the object can do are called *Methods*. In our example, a Student has two *Attributes* Student-Name and Student-Id-Number; and two *Methods,* Tell-Name and Tell-Id-Number.

In a system involving students, we would expect to have many different students. For example, if a university has 18,000 students, we would have 18,000 objects - one object per student. In OO terminology, each student object is called an *Instance*. We would have 18,000 *instances* of Student. We would write a *Class Program* to represent the Students in this system. This *class program* will contain code that defines the *Attributes,* Student-Name and Student-Id-Number.

Also, this program will have procedural code to do the processing necessary for the two *Methods*, Tell-Name and Tell-Id-Number.

It appears then that we can have a *Class Program* that represents the Student group and we will then create *instances* to represent each student as we do whatever processing is called for. This terminology is important. In OO terms, we design and write a Class Program that represents a collection of things such as Students, Customers, or Reservations. The term *Class* is used to describe the group.

As we do the processing, we create *instances* of Student, Customer or Reservation as needed. The term *Instance* refers to individual items in the group.

Writing A Class Program

In Chapter 4, a small COBOL program was developed to compute present value. This program was named MYSECOND. In this section, two very small programs named MYTHIRD and MYFOURTH will created. MYFOURTH is a class program.

The relationship between MYTHIRD and MYFOURTH is shown in Figure 5.1. These two

```
        MYTHIRD                    MYFOURTH
  1.  Accept Future-Value
  2.  Accept Interest-Rate
  3.  Accept Number-of-Years
                          4.  Compute Present-Value
  5.  Display Present-Value
```

Figure 5.1: The Relationship Between MYTHIRD and MYFOURTH

programs working together will do the same thing as MYSECOND did in the previous chapter. MYTHIRD will accept the Future-Value, Interest-Rate, and Number-of-Years, then "ask" MYFOURTH to compute the Present-Value. MYFOURTH will compute the Present-Value and "tell" MYTHIRD. MYTHIRD will then display the Present-Value.

From a user's perspective, these two programs together will function the same as the single program, MYSECOND in Chapter 4. The screen input and output is identical.

To write MYTHIRD, you can either make a copy of MYSECOND.CBL, rename it MYTHIRD.CBL, then make the changes shown boldface in Figure 5.2. Or you can key the program in from scratch. Either way, use the Animator as described in Chapter 4, and then save the program as MYTHIRD.CBL. The complete listing of MYTHIRD is shown in Figure 5.2.

```
Program-Id. MYTHIRD.
CLASS-CONTROL.
    MYFOURTH is Class "MYFOURTH".
01  Future-Value    Pic 9(5).
01  Interest-Rate   Pic V99999.
01  Number-Of-Years Pic 9(3).
01  Present-Value   Pic Z,ZZ9.99.
01  Are-We-Thru     Pic X(3).
    88 We-Are-Thru    Values "YES" "Yes" "yes".
Procedure Division.
    Display "This program computes Present Value"
    Perform until We-Are-Thru
        Display "Enter the Future Value (whole dollar amount)"
        Accept Future-Value
        Display "Enter the Interest Rate (.nnnnn)"
        Accept Interest-Rate
        Display "Enter the Number of Years in the future"
        Accept Number-of-Years
        Invoke MYFOURTH "ComputePresentValue"
            Using Future-Value, Interest-Rate, Number-Of-Years
            Returning Present-Value
        Display "The Present Value is: ", Present-Value
        Display "Enter 'YES' to Stop, any key to continue"
        Accept Are-We-Thru
    End-Perform
    Stop Run.
```

Figure 5.2: Listing Of Mythird.Cbl

Notice that MYTHIRD is simply a copy of MYSECOND with two important differences that are **boldfaced** in the listing. First, following the Program-Id clause, a CLASS-CONTROL clause has been added to name the class program that MYTHIRD will interact with; in this example it is MYFOURTH. The second change is the Compute statement has been replaced with an INVOKE verb. This Invoke statement will execute the method named "ComputePresentValue" in the class program MYFOURTH.

Next, you will enter and save the program named MYFOURTH.CBL, again using the Animator. The listing for MYFOURTH is shown in Figure 5.3.

```
$set mfoo
Class-id. MYFOURTH.
Method-id. "ComputePresentValue".
linkage section.
01  Future-Value-ls     Pic 9(5).
01  Interest-Rate-ls    Pic V99999.
01  Number-Of-Years-ls  Pic 9(3).
01  Present-Value-ls    Pic Z,ZZ9.99.
Procedure Division
    USING  Future-Value-ls, Interest-Rate-ls, Number-Of-Years-ls
    Returning Present-Value-ls.
    Compute Present-Value-ls Rounded =  Future-Value-ls /
        (1 + Interest-Rate-ls) ** Number-Of-Years-ls
    exit method.
end method "ComputePresentValue".
end class MYFOURTH.
```

Figure 5.3: Listing Of Myfourth.Cbl

MYFOURTH is a Class Program. Boldface has been used to indicate the new OO statements. The first line "$set mfoo" is a Micro Focus compiler directive that tells the compiler this is an OO class program. The **Class-id** clause simply names the Class and is similar to a Program-id clause. The **Method-id** header indicates the beginning of the method named "ComputePresentValue". The next to the last line in the program, **end method**, is a scope terminator that marks the end of the method. The **exit method** statement is similar to the exit program statement. It returns to the statement following the Invoke, which in this case is in program MYTHIRD. Finally, the **end class** clause indicates the physical end of the class program.

The Linkage Section serves the same purpose in a Class Program as it docs in a traditional procedural program. When you use the Call statement to execute a subprogram, the subprogram can have a Linkage Section to provide access to data items residing in the calling program. Similarly, the Linkage Section in a method provides access to data that resides in the invoking program. In this case, the method "ComputePresentValue" can access the data elements that reside in MYTHIRD: Future-Value, Interest-Rate, Number-Of-Years, and Present-Value. The suffix "LS" has been added simply to indicate these are linkage section data items. Notice that in the PROCEDURE DIVISION header, we also specify the names of the these data items.

The actual Procedure Division is quite short, but then it only needs to compute Present-Value. The Compute statement is identical to the one in MYSECOND.

To Load MYTHIRD and MYFOURTH:

1. Launch the Browser.

2. Click **FILE|Open/New Project.**

3. Enter "MYFIRST.PRJ" in the Open Project File window.

4. Click **FILE|OPEN…** and key in "MYTHIRD.CBL" in the Open File window.

5. Click **FILE|OPEN…** and key in "MYFOURTH.CBL" in the Open File window. Your screen should look similar to Figure 5.4. The Browser window has four panes. The three small ones across the top are named Classes, Files, and Sections/Methods. The large pane in the bottom half of the window is for our program text.

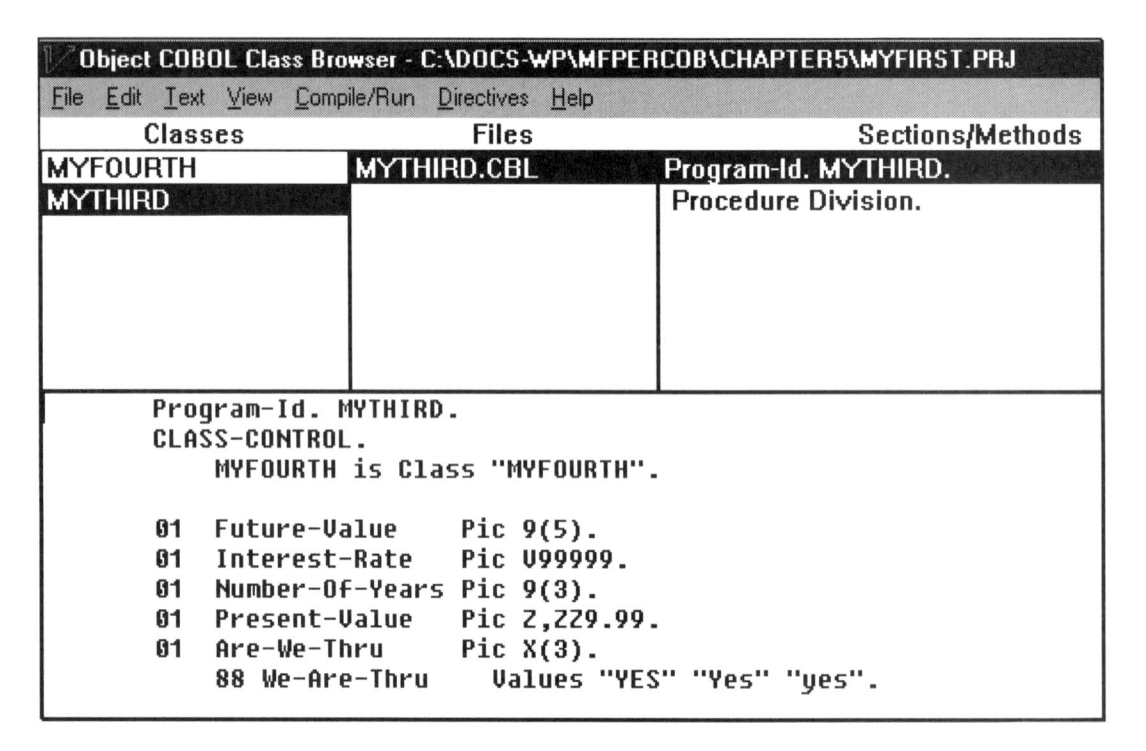

Figure 5.4: Browser Window With MYTHIRD & MYFOURTH Loaded

6. You control which part of which program is displayed in the main pane. To illustrate, click MYTHIRD in the Classes pane.

7. Next, click the Working-Storage Section in the Sections/Methods pane.

8. Click the Procedure Division in the Sections/Methods pane. Notice how the code in the main pane at the bottom reflects the section you have highlighted in the Sections/Methods pane. When Working-Storage Section is highlighted, the code in this section is displayed. When the Procedure Division is highlighted, the code in the Procedure Division is displayed.

9. You can change the way the program is displayed by clicking **View** then selecting one of the view options from the pull-down menu. For example, click **View|File Only**, then click the filename MYTHIRD.CBL in the Sections/Methods pane to view the entire program.

To Compile MYTHIRD and MYFOURTH:

1. Click MYFOURTH in the Classes pane. Because MYFOURTH is executed from MYTHIRD, MYFOURTH is compiled first.

2. Click **Compile/Run|Compile** or press the F2 key.

3. Click MYTHIRD in the Classes pane.

4. Click **Compile/Run|Compile** or press the F2 key.

5. If you encounter syntax errors, they will appear slightly differently than errors displayed by the Animator. The Browser displays syntax error messages in the Sections/Methods pane. As you click these messages, the statement containing the syntax error is highlighted in the main pane. Correct errors if you have them.

To Execute MYTHIRD and MYFOURTH:

1. Click MYTHIRD in the Classes pane. Because MYTHIRD invokes MYFOURTH, this program is the one to be executed.

2. Click **Compile/Run|Animate** or press the F4 key.

3. Click Yes on the Save Changes message.

1. You have now launched the Animator (from the Browser). Your screen should look similar to Figure 5.5.

```
Edit+Execute:C:\DOCS-WP\MFPERCOB\CHAPTER5\MYTHIRD.INT (mythird.cbl)
10      88 We-Are-Thru     Values "YES" "Yes" "yes".
11 Procedure Division.
12      Display "This program computes Present Value"
13      Perform until We-Are-Thru
14          Display "Enter the Future Value (whole dollar amount)"
15          Accept Future-Value
16          Display "Enter the Interest Rate (.nnnnn)"
17          Accept Interest-Rate
18          Display "Enter the Number of Years in the future"
19          Accept Number-of-Years
20          Invoke MYFOURTH "ComputePresentValue"
21              Using Future-Value, Interest-Rate, Number-Of-Years
22              Returning Present-Value
23          Display "The Present Value is: ", Present-Value
24          Display "Enter 'YES' to Stop, any key to continue"
25          Accept Are-We-Thru
26      End-Perform
27      Stop Run.
......................end of text.........................
```

Figure 5.5: Animating MYTHIRD and MYFOURTH

5. Click the Step button ▨, or press Ctrl+S to begin executing one statement at a time.

6. When prompted, enter "1075" Future Value, ".075" Interest Rate, and "1" Number of Years.

7. When you get to the Invoke statement, execute it and then notice you are now animating MYFOURTH.

8. Continue stepping through the program. Your output should look similar to that in Chapter 4.

9. When prompted enter "Yes" at the Are You Through message.

10. Close the Animator.

11. Close the Browser.

To Learn More

There are several opportunities for you to learn more about Object COBOL. A good place to start is the OO Tutorials supplied with the Micro Focus Personal COBOL for Windows system.

To access these Tutorials:

1. Click **Help|Online Tutorials and Reference**

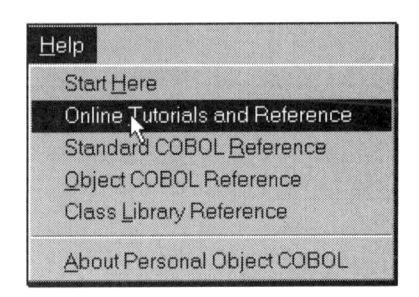

2. Click **Tutorials.**

3. Click **Beginning Tutorials.**

5-10

Bibliography

Arranga, E. And F. Coyle. <u>Object-Oriented COBOL</u>, SIGS Publications, Inc., 1996.

Chapin, N. <u>Standard Object-Oriented COBOL</u>, John Wiley & Sons, 1997.

Coad. P. <u>Object Models: Strategies, Patterns, and Applications</u>. Prentice-Hall, 1995.

Doke, E.R. and Hardgrave B. <u>An Introduction to Object COBOL</u>, John Wiley & Sons, 1997.

Firesmith, D.G. <u>Object-Oriented Requirements Analysis and Logical Design</u>, John Wiley & Sons, 1993.

Jacobson, I. Et al. <u>Object-Oriented Software Engineering: A Use Case Driven Approach</u>, Addison-Wesley, 1992.

Levey, R. <u>Re-Engineering COBOL With Objects</u>, McGraw-Hill, 1995.

Obin, R. <u>Object-Orientation: An Introduction for COBOL Programmers</u>, second edition, Micro Focus Publishing, 1995.

Price, W. <u>Elements of Object-Oriented COBOL</u>, Object-Z Publishing, 1997.

Rabin, S. "Transitioning Information Systems COBOL Developers into Object COBOL Technicians," <u>Object Magazine</u>, January 1995, pp. 71 - 75.

Rumbaugh, J. et al. <u>Object-Oriented Modeling and Design</u>, Prentice-Hall, 1991.

Satzinger. J and T. Orvik. <u>Object-Oriented Approach: Concepts, Modeling, and Systems Development</u>, Boyd & Fraser, 1996.

Shlaer, S. And S.J. Mellor. <u>Object Lifecycles: Modeling the World in States</u>, Prentice-Hall, 1992.

Taylor, D.A. <u>Object-Oriented Systems: Planning and Implementation</u>, John Wiley & Sons, 1992.

Taylor, D.A. <u>Object-Oriented Technology: A Manager's Guide</u>, Addison-Wesley Publishing Company, 1990.

Topper, A. <u>Object-Oriented Development in COBOL</u>, McGraw-Hill, 1995.

Yourdon, E. <u>Object-Oriented Systems Design: An Integrated Approach</u>, Yourdon Press Prentice-Hall, 1994.

Chapter 6

Additional Features of Personal COBOL

Personal Dialog System

The Class Library

Accept and Display Statements

The Screen Section

This chapter describes additional features of the Personal COBOL for Windows system. A summary of the Personal Dialog System, the Class Library and screen input-output is presented. This chapter does not provide an in-depth description of these features, but it gives you a good overview.

Personal Dialog System

The Micro Focus Personal Dialog System ™ is a Graphical User Interface (GUI) tool included with the Personal COBOL for Windows system. You can use the Personal Dialog System (PDS) to create screens, and then incorporate these screens into your COBOL program. In fact, you can use the PDS to generate screen prototypes to evaluate alternative screen designs.

The PDS can be used to define your application's windows, along with the data fields and descriptive text in these windows. You can also define buttons in the window and then write procedural (COBOL) code to describe the behavior of the window and its components. All of these window specifications are stored in a file called a screenset. Screenset files have a suffix of ".GS."

A COBOL program can then use the GUI screen by accessing the screen definition through the PDS run-time software. Data to be input or output in the window is passed through the run-time software.

If you would like to learn more about PDS, launch the PDS User Guide then click **Quick Tour**. This will take you through the steps to create a simple program using a GUI that you develop. In addition, there are several programs included in the \SAMPLES directory that use PDS code.

The Class Library

The Micro Focus Personal COBOL for Windows system is supplied with a library of Class Programs. You can access this library and use these classes as you wish.

To Learn About the Class Library:

1. Launch the Browser.

2. Click **Help|Class Library Reference** as shown in Figure 6.1.

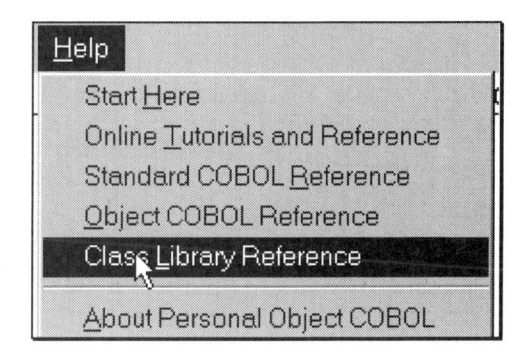

Figure 6.1: Accessing Class Library Reference

3. Your screen should appear similar to Figure 6.2.

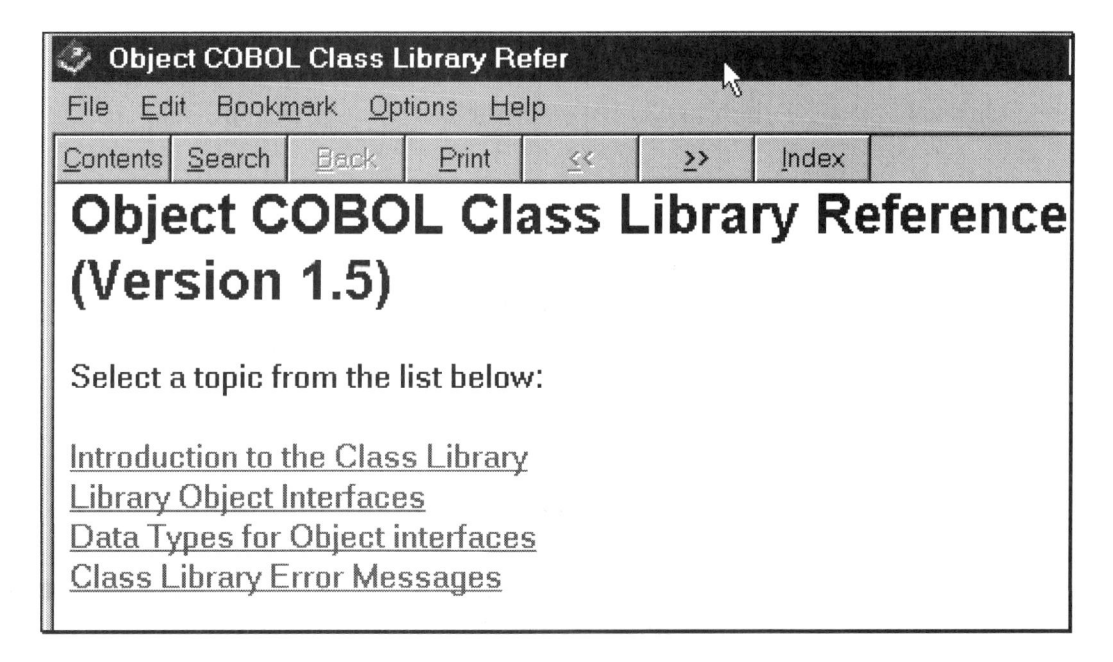

Figure 6.2: Class Library Reference Screen

From this screen, you can explore the interfaces to the various classes contained in the library. If you wish, you can examine the source code of any class by looking in the \CLASSLIB subdirectory in the \PCOBWIN directory.

Accept and Display Statements

In the PC environment, the ACCEPT and DISPLAY statements are used for screen input and output. When coupled with the Screen Section definition in the Data Division (see the next section), a powerful interactive interface can be developed. Although this interface is text-based as opposed to GUI, it is an effective technique for screen input and output.

The Personal COBOL for Windows system includes a run-time module that gives you expanded ACCEPT and DISPLAY syntax. This run-time system is called ADIS which is an acronym for Accept/DISplay. ADIS also enables you to detect function key presses, which can can be used to enhance your application's interface.

The ACCEPT verb is used to read data from the screen. You can use one of two basic formats:

```
1. ACCEPT data-item

2. ACCEPT data-item AT LINE nn COLUMN nn
```

The first form will read data from the current cursor location. The second form reads data beginning at the line and column specified. Usually there are 24 lines and 80 columns on a screen.

There are additional options with the ACCEPT verb such as "WITH BLINK" and "BEEP."

To Learn More About the ACCEPT Statement:

1. Launch either the Animator or the Browser.

2. Click **Help|Standard COBOL Reference**.

3. Click **COBOL Source Syntax**.

4. Click **COBOL Verbs.**

5. Click **ACCEPT** to see the syntax and various options.

The DISPLAY verb displays data on the screen. Similar to ACCEPT, the DISPLAY statement has two forms:

```
1. DISPLAY data-item

2. DISPLAY data-item AT LINE nn COLUMN nn
```

The first form will display the data at the current cursor location. The second form displays the data at a specified line and column on the screen.

To Learn More About the DISPLAY Statement:

1. Launch either the Animator or the Browser.

2. Click **Help|Standard COBOL Reference**.

3. Click **COBOL Source Syntax**

4. Click **COBOL Verbs.**

5. Click DISPLAY to see the syntax and various options.

The Screen Section

The Data Division for the ANSI-9X COBOL standard includes a section called the Screen Section. The Micro Focus Personal COBOL system also includes this feature. The purpose of this section is to describe screens to be used for input or output or both. Using the Screen Section enables you to describe and display screen informationmore easily than by using the Accept and Display statements previously described.

To illustrate the use of the screen section, program MYSECOND has been modified to include a Screen Section. The modified program is named MYFIFTH and is listed in Figure 6-3.

The Screen Section in MYFIFTH is highlighted in boldface. There is a single 01 level group item named Instructions, followed by several level 05 elementary items which define the values to be displayed along with their screen locations (line and column). The `Erase EOS` clause at the end of the first elementary item erases the screen. Figure 6-4 shows the screen displayed when MYFIFTH is executed. This screen is slightly different than the screen displayed by MYSECOND, but it has the same information.

The third statement in the procedure division `Display Instructions` displays the screen that is described in the Screen Section. The remaining Accept and Display statements have been modified to specify a screen location. These modifications are shown in boldface.

```
Program-Id. MYFIFTH.
Data Division.
Working-Storage Section.
01  Future-Value    Pic 9(5).
01  Interest-Rate   Pic V99999.
01  Number-Of-Years Pic 9(3).
01  Present-Value   Pic ZZ,ZZ9.99.
01  Are-We-Thru     Pic X(3).
    88 We-Are-Thru    Values "YES" "Yes" "yes".
Screen Section.
01  Instructions.
    05 Value "This program computes Present Value" Line 10 Col 9
       Erase EOS.
    05 Value "Enter the Future Value(whole $),   " Line 12 Col 9.
    05 Value "Then the Interest Rate,            " Line 13 Col 9.
    05 Value "Then the Number of Years.          " Line 14 Col 9.
    05 Value "Future Value (whole dollars):"       Line 16 Col 9.
    05 Value "Interest Rate:."                     Line 17 Col 9.
    05 Value "Number of Years:"                    Line 18 Col 9.
    05 Value "The Present Value is:"               Line 20 Col 9.
    05 Value "Enter 'YES' to stop, any other key to continue:"
                                                   Line 22 Col 9.
Procedure Division.
    Perform until We-Are-Thru
        Initialize Future-Value, Interest-Rate, Number-of-Years
        Display Instructions
        Accept Future-Value    Line 16 Col 38
        Accept Interest-Rate   Line 17 Col 24
        Accept Number-of-Years Line 18 Col 25
        Compute Present-Value Rounded =
            Future-Value / (1 + Interest-Rate) ** Number-Of-Years
        Display Present-Value  Line 20 Col 31
        Accept Are-We-Thru     Line 22 Col 57
    End-Perform
    Stop Run.
```

Figure 6.3: MYFIFTH Program Using a Screen Section

To Learn More About the Screen Section:

   1. Launch either the Animator or the Browser.

   2. Click **Help|Standard COBOL Reference**.

   3. Click **COBOL Source Syntax**.

   4. Click **COBOL Program Structure**.

   5. Click **Screen Description**.

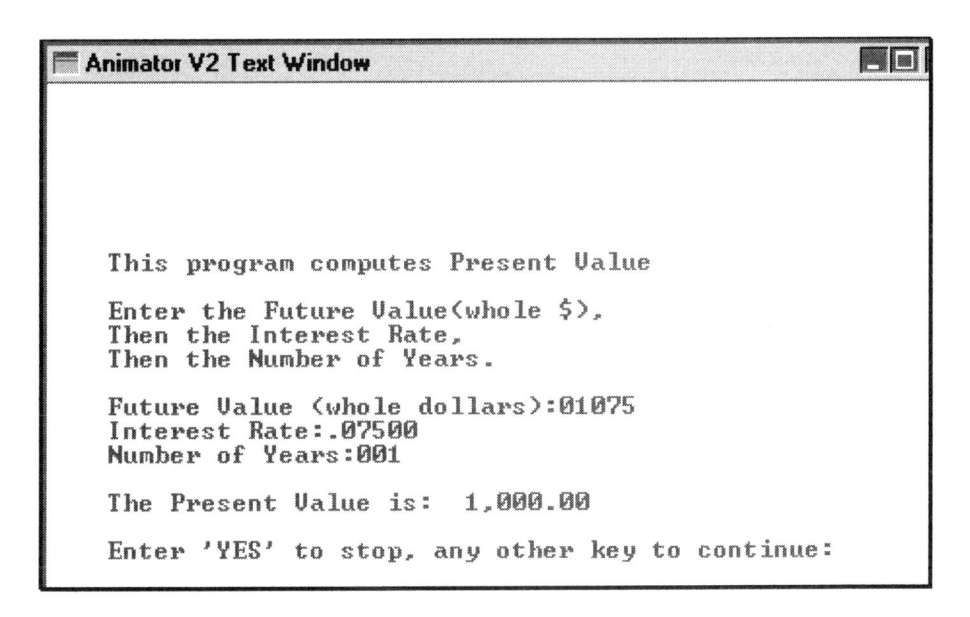

```
 Animator V2 Text Window                          ■□



        This program computes Present Value

        Enter the Future Value(whole $),
        Then the Interest Rate,
        Then the Number of Years.

        Future Value (whole dollars):01075
        Interest Rate:.07500
        Number of Years:001

        The Present Value is:  1,000.00

        Enter 'YES' to stop, any other key to continue:
```

Figure 6.4: Output from MYFIFTH Program

Chapter 7

File Processing

Sequential File Processing

Printing Reports

This chapter describes sequential file processing and report printing. A sequential file is created using the Animator and a small COBOL program is used to illustrate accessing this file. Next, the program is expanded to print a report.

Sequential File Processing

In this section we will create a small sequential file using the Animator, and then write a simple COBOL program to read the file and display its contents.

The data file is named "STUDENT.DAT" and consists of data records for four students. Each record has two fields: STUDENT-NAME in columns 1 through 15, and STUDENT-ID in columns 16 through 24, as shown below.

```
--------------- Columns ---------------
            1                 2
123456789012345678901234

Scott Petrie   499663232
Cliff Segrist  445860508
Mark Hains     494742355
Doug Davis     490694854
```

To Create This File:

1. Launch the Animator.

2. Enter the data as shown in Figure 7.1, being careful to begin the student name field in column 1 and the Id field in column 16. Press Shift+Tab to move the cursor from the default column 8 to column 1. Notice that the status bar shows the cursor location and tells you whether the Insert (Ins), CapsLock (Caps) and NumLock (Num) modes are activated.

3. Click **File|Save As . .**

4. Enter the filename "STUDENT.DAT" to save the file.

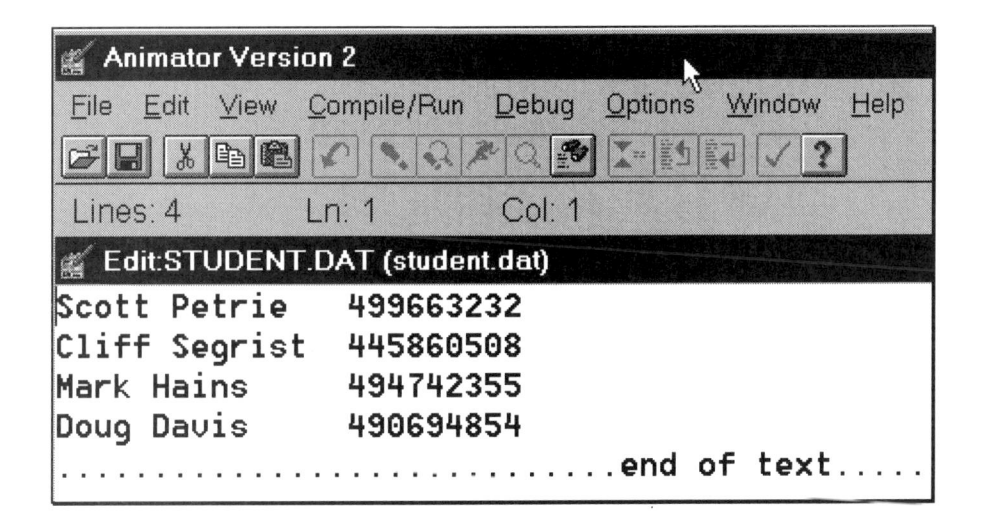

Figure 7.1: Entering the Data for STUDENT..DAT File

Next, you will enter a short COBOL program that will read this data file and display its contents.

To Enter the Program MYSIXTH:

1. If you have not done so, launch the Animator.

2. Click **File|New.**

3. Enter the program named MYSIXTH as shown in Figure 7.2.

   This program includes all of the division and section headers such as "IDENTIFICATION DIVISION" and "DATA DIVISION." If you wish, you may omit these to reduce the amount of typing. The program will execute correctly without these entries.

   Notice the SELECT statement in this program:

   ```
   SELECT STUDENT-FILE ASSIGN TO "STUDENT.DAT"
          Organization is Line Sequential.
   ```

   There are a couple of points to emphasize here. First, the DOS file name of the input data file, "STUDENT.DAT" is specified in this clause. You can specify the complete DOS path if you wish. For example, if you want to have the data file on drive A, you would enter "A:STUDENT.DAT" instead of just "STUDENT.DAT." If you do not specify the path, the default drive and directory will be assumed.

Second, the ORGANIZATION clause specifies "Line Sequential." This organization is used for sequential files whose records terminate with two special characters, a carriage return and line feed. These two characters, which indicate the end of a record, are typically added to text files created by text editors such as the one used by the Animator. If you create a data file using a word processor and then save it as a DOS text file, it will have the carriage return and line feed characters as record terminators. You will need to include the "Organization is Line Sequential" clause in this case. Sequential files created by another program will not have the carriage return and line feed characters as record terminators. For such files specify "Organization is Sequential" or omit the clause entirely since sequential is the default value.

```
Identification Division.
Program-Id. MYSIXTH.
Environment Division.
Input-Output Section.
File-Control.
    Select Student-File Assign To "Student.Dat"
        Organization is Line Sequential.
Data Division.
File Section.
Fd  Student-File.
01  Student-Record.
    05  Student-Name    Pic X(15).
    05  Student-Id      Pic X(9).
Working-Storage Section.
01  End-Of-File-Sw      Pic X(3).
    88  End-Of-File Value "Yes".
Procedure Division.
    Open Input Student-File
    Perform Read-A-Record
    Perform Until End-Of-File
        Perform Display-A-Record
        Perform Read-A-Record
    End-Perform
    Close Student-File
    Stop Run.
Read-A-Record.
    Read Student-File
        At End Move "Yes" To End-Of-File-Sw
    End-Read.
Display-A-Record.
    Display Student-Name, Student-Id.
```

Figure 7.2: MYSIXTH Program Listing

4. Click **File|Save As..**

5. Enter "MYSIXTH.CBL" to save the file.

6. Click **File|Open For Execution**.

7. Enter "MYSIXTH.CBL" to reload the program in execution mode.

8. Compile the program by either clicking the Check button █, or by selecting **Compile/Run|Compile Program**. If you encounter any compiler-generated error messages, carefully check your program against Figure 7.2 and correct any differences.

9. When you have an error-free compile, run the program by clicking either the Run button █ or **Compile/Run|Run**. As the program executes, the data from the file STUDENT.DAT will be displayed on the output screen.

Printing Reports

You will now make a copy of MYSIXTH.CBL and modify it so that it will print the student data onto a report.

1. Launch the Animator.

2. Click **File|Open for Execution**, and enter "MYSIXTH.CBL" to load this program.

3. Click **File|Save As . .**

4. Enter "MYSVNTH.CBL" to save the program under the name MYSEVNTH. The complete MYSEVNTH program is listed in Figure 7.3. The changes made to MYSIXTH.CBL which are indicated in boldface are outlined in steps 5 through 12.

5. Change the program name to "MYSEVNTH."

6. Add a SELECT statement for the Report-File. The code in Figure 7.3 specifies that the report will be saved in a file named "OUTPUT.DAT". If you wish, you can instead specify "PRINTER" to print directly to a printer.

7. Code the FD (file definition clause) for the Report-File.

8. Add the record definition for Print-Record immediately following the FD.

9. Code the four entries for Detail-Line at the beginning of the working-storage section.

10. In the Procedure Division, add Report-File to the Open statement.

11. Add Report-File to the Close statement.

12. Replace the Display statement in the paragraph Display-A-Record with the three new lines of code shown in Figure 7.3. These statements format and write a detail line for each student record.

```
Identification Division.
Program-Id. MYSEVNTH.
Environment Division.
Input-Output Section.
File-Control.
    Select Student-File Assign To "Student.Dat"
        Organization Is Line Sequential.
    Select Report-File Assign To "Output.Dat".
Data Division.
Fd  Student-File.
01  Student-Record.
    05  Student-Name    Pic X(15).
    05  Student-Id      Pic X(9).
Fd  Report-File.
01  Print-Record        Pic X(50).
Working-Storage Section.
01  Detail-Line.
    05  Student-Name-DL Pic X(15).
    05                  Pic X(5) Value Spaces.
    05  Student-Id-DL   Pic X(9).
01  End-Of-File-Sw      Pic X(3).
    88  End-Of-File Value "Yes".
Procedure Division.
    Open Input  Student-File
            Output Report-File
    Perform Read-A-Record
    Perform Until End-Of-File
        Perform Display-A-Record
        Perform Read-A-Record
    End-Perform
    Close Student-File Report-File
    Stop Run.
Read-A-Record.
    Read Student-File
        At End Move "Yes" To End-Of-File-Sw
    End-Read.
Display-A Record.
    Move Student-Name To Student-Name-Dl
    Move Student-Id   To Student-Id-Dl
    Write Print-Record From Detail-Line After Advancing 1.
```

Figure 7.3 MYSEVNTH Program Listing

13. Click **File|Save** to save the program.

14. Compile the program by either clicking the Check button ☑, or by selecting **Compile/Run|Compile Program**. If you encounter any compiler-generated error messages, carefully check your program against Figure 7.3 and correct any differences.

15. When you have an error-free compile, run the program by clicking either the Run button 🏃 or **Compile/Run|Run**

If you assigned the report file to "PRINTER" your output report went directly to the printer. If you assigned the report file to OUTPUT.DAT, this file is created when the program executes. You can view this file using any text editor program (such as NotePad) or if you wish, you can use the Animator. To use the Animator:

1. Launch the Animator if it is not already loaded.

2. Click **File|Open for Edit . . ..**

3. Enter "OUTPUT.DAT" as the file name. You should see a window similar to Figure 7.4. This is the report file produced by MYSEVNTH program.

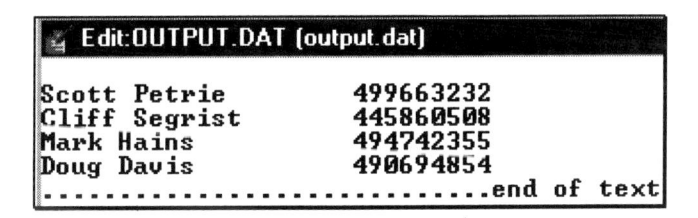

Figure 7-4: Listing of OUTPUT.DAT File

4. Click **File|Exit** to exit the Animator.

Appendix A

Troubleshooting

The COBOL Environment

Compiler Messages

Runtime Messages

Getting Additional Help

This appendix is included to help if you have problems with installing or using the Micro Focus Personal COBOL for Windows system. The first section describes the COBOL environment variables required by the system. Then both compiler and run-time messages are discussed. The last section offers suggestions for obtaining additional assistance.

If you are having problems installing or using the Personal COBOL system, the first thing you should do is click on the **README** icon in the Personal COBOL Program group. There are several common difficulties described along with suggested solutions.

The COBOL Environment

The Personal COBOL system requires the following environment variables. These statements should have been added to your AUTOEXEC.BAT and CONFIG.SYS files during installation. If your System does not work correctly, you should check these statements.

To check the environment variables, go to the DOS prompt, type "SET", and press enter. The following environment variables are required by the Personal COBOL System (the following assumes that you installed the system into the directory \PCOBWIN; if you installed into a different directory, substitute its name for \PCOBWIN):

```
PATH=C:\PCOBWIN; (plus additional paths)
COBDIR=C:\PCOBWIN
COBHNF=C:\PCOBWIN
COBCPY=C:\PCOBWIN\CLASSLIB
DSGDIR=C:\PCOBWIN
COBSW=+p3/S14000
```

There is a batch file named PCOBENV.BAT in the \PCOBWIN directory that will set the variables for you if needed. These environment variables must be set before Windows is started or they will be ignored.

In addition, the FILES setting in your CONFIG.SYS file must be at least 100 and BUFFERS must be at least 10.

Compiler Messages

Whenever the Compiler detects a syntax error, it displays a message. This message includes a brief description of the error plus a number. For example, if you use a data item name in the Procedure Division that you have not defined in the Data Division (or have spelled it differently in the Data Division), the Compiler will display the message:

        12-S   Operand .... Not Declared

Usually you will quickly see how to correct the problem. If you need an additional explanation of the message:

1. Click **Help|Standard COBOL Reference** from either the Browser or Animator.

2. Scroll down until you see the heading "COBOL Messages".

3. Click **Syntax Errors**.

4. Click the error number you wish to investigate.

Run-time Messages

A *Compiler Message* is one that is produced by the system during the compilation or checking process. A *Run-time message* will occur while your program is being executed. These messages are displayed by the Run-time System (RTS). To investigate run-time messages:

1. Click **Help|Standard COBOL Reference** from either the Browser or Animator.

2. Scroll down until you see the heading "COBOL Messages".

3. Click **RTS Errors**.

4. Click the error number you wish to investigate.

Getting Additional Help

There is a Micro Focus forum on Compuserve (GO MICROFOCUS).

Micro Focus has a Website at http://WWW.MICROFOCUS.COM. You can also send E-mail to MFPUBLG@MICROFOCUS.COM.

Appendix B

Program Listings

MYFIRST
MYSECOND
MYTHIRD
MYFOURTH
MYFIFTH
MYSIXTH
MYSEVNTH

MYFIRST

```
Identification Division.
Program-Id. Myfirst.
Data Division.
Working-Storage Section.
01  A-Value    Pic 9(3).
01  The-Result Pic 9(5).
01  Are-We-Thru Pic x(3).
Procedure Division.
    Display "This program accepts a value, then displays"
    Display "the square of the value."
    Perform until are-we-thru = "yes" or "YES" or "Yes"
        display "enter the value"
        accept a-value
        compute the-result = a-value * a-value
        display the-result
        display "Enter 'YES' if you are through"
        accept are-we-thru
    end-perform
    stop run.
```

MYSECOND

```
Program-Id. MYSECOND.
01  Future-Value    Pic 9(5).
01  Interest-Rate   Pic V99999.
01  Number-Of-Years Pic 9(3).
01  Present-Value   Pic Z,ZZ9.99.
01  Are-We-Thru     Pic X(3).
    88 We-Are-Thru    Values "YES" "Yes" "yes".
Procedure Division.
    Display "This program computes Present Value"
    Perform until We-Are-Thru
        Display "Enter the Future Value (whole dollar amount)"
        Accept Future-Value
        Display "Enter the Interest Rate (.nnnnn)"
        Accept Interest-Rate
        Display "Enter the Number of Years in the future"
        Accept Number-of-Years
        Compute Present-Value Rounded =
            Future-Value / (1 + Interest-Rate) ** Number-Of-Years
        Display "The Present Value is: ", Present-Value
        Display "Enter 'YES' to Stop, any key to continue"
        Accept Are-We-Thru
    End-Perform
    Stop Run.
```

MYTHIRD

```
Program-Id. MYTHIRD.
CLASS-CONTROL.
    MYFOURTH is Class "MYFOURTH".
01  Future-Value    Pic 9(5).
01  Interest-Rate   Pic V99999.
01  Number-Of-Years Pic 9(3).
01  Present-Value   Pic Z,ZZ9.99.
01  Are-We-Thru     Pic X(3).
    88 We-Are-Thru    Values "YES" "Yes" "yes".
Procedure Division.
    Display "This program computes Present Value"
    Perform until We-Are-Thru
        Display "Enter the Future Value (whole dollar amount)"
        Accept Future-Value
        Display "Enter the Interest Rate (.nnnnn)"
        Accept Interest-Rate
        Display "Enter the Number of Years in the future"
        Accept Number-of-Years
        Invoke MYFOURTH "ComputePresentValue"
            Using Future-Value, Interest-Rate, Number-Of-Years
            Returning Present-Value
        Display "The Present Value is: ", Present-Value
        Display "Enter 'YES' to Stop, any key to continue"
        Accept Are-We-Thru
    End-Perform
    Stop Run.
```

MYFOURTH

```
$set mfoo
Class-id. MYFOURTH.
*Class-control.
*      MYFOURTH is class "myfourth".
Method-id. "ComputePresentValue".
linkage section.
01  Future-Value-ls   Pic 9(5).
01  Interest-Rate-ls  Pic V99999.
01  Number-Of-Years-ls Pic 9(3).
01  Present-Value-ls  Pic Z,ZZ9.99.
Procedure Division
    USING  Future-Value-ls, Interest-Rate-ls, Number-Of-Years-ls
    Returning Present-Value-ls.
    Compute Present-Value-ls Rounded =  Future-Value-ls /
        (1 + Interest-Rate-ls) ** Number-Of-Years-ls
    exit method.
end method "ComputePresentValue".
end class MYFOURTH.
```

MYFIFTH

```
Program-Id. MYFIFTH.
01  Future-Value    Pic 9(5).
01  Interest-Rate   Pic V99999.
01  Number-Of-Years Pic 9(3).
01  Present-Value   Pic ZZ,ZZ9.99.
01  Are-We-Thru     Pic X(3).
    88 We-Are-Thru    Values "YES" "Yes" "yes".
Screen Section.
01  Instructions.
    05 Value "This program computes Present Value" Line 10 Col 9
        Erase EOS.
    05 Value "Enter the Future Value(whole $),    " Line 12 Col 9.
    05 Value "Then the Interest Rate,            " Line 13 Col 9.
    05 Value "Then the Number of Years.          " Line 14 COl 9.
    05 Value "Future Value (whole dollars):"       Line 16 Col 9.
    05 Value "Interest Rate:."                     Line 17 Col 9.
    05 Value "Number of Years:"                    Line 18 Col 9.
    05 Value "The Present Value is:"               Line 20 Col 9.
    05 Value "Enter 'YES' to stop, any other key to continue:"
                                                   Line 22 Col 9.
Procedure Division.
    Perform until We-Are-Thru
        Initialize Future-Value, Interest-Rate, Number-of-Years
        Display Instructions
        Accept Future-Value    Line 16 Col 38
        Accept Interest-Rate   Line 17 Col 24
        Accept Number-of-Years Line 18 Col 25
        Compute Present-Value Rounded =
            Future-Value / (1 + Interest-Rate) ** Number-Of-Years
        Display Present-Value Line 20 Col 31
        Accept Are-We-Thru Line 22 Col 57
    End-Perform
    Stop Run.
```

MYSIXTH

```
IDENTIFICATION DIVISION.
Program-Id. MYSIXTH.
Environment Division.
Input-Output Section.
File-Control.
    SELECT STUDENT-FILE ASSIGN TO "STUDENT.DAT"
        Organization is Line Sequential.
DATA DIVISION.
FD  STUDENT-FILE.
01  STUDENT-RECORD.
    05  STUDENT-NAME    PIC X(15).
    05  STUDENT-ID      PIC X(9).

WORKING-STORAGE SECTION.
01  END-OF-FILE-SW      PIC X(3).
    88  END-OF-FILE VALUE "YES".
PROCEDURE DIVISION.
    OPEN INPUT STUDENT-FILE
    PERFORM READ-A-RECORD
    PERFORM UNTIL END-OF-FILE
        PERFORM DISPLAY-A-RECORD
        PERFORM READ-A-RECORD
    END-PERFORM
    STOP RUN.
READ-A-RECORD.
    READ STUDENT-FILE
        AT END MOVE "YES" TO END-OF-FILE-SW
    END-READ.
DISPLAY-A-RECORD.
    DISPLAY STUDENT-NAME, STUDENT-ID.
```

MYSEVNTH

```
IDENTIFICATION DIVISION.
Program-Id. MYSEVNTH.
Environment Division.
Input-Output Section.
File-Control.
    SELECT STUDENT-FILE ASSIGN TO "STUDENT.DAT"
        Organization is Line Sequential.
    SELECT REPORT-FILE ASSIGN TO "OUTPUT.DAT".
DATA DIVISION.
FILE SECTION.
FD  STUDENT-FILE.
01  STUDENT-RECORD.
    05  STUDENT-NAME    PIC X(15).
    05  STUDENT-ID      PIC X(9).
FD  REPORT-FILE.
01  PRINT-RECORD        PIC X(50).

WORKING-STORAGE SECTION.
01  DETAIL-LINE.
    05  STUDENT-NAME-DL PIC X(15).
    05                  PIC X(5) VALUE SPACES.
    05  STUDENT-ID-DL   PIC X(9).
01  END-OF-FILE-SW      PIC X(3).
    88  END-OF-FILE VALUE "YES".
PROCEDURE DIVISION.
    OPEN INPUT   STUDENT-FILE
         OUTPUT REPORT-FILE
    PERFORM READ-A-RECORD
    PERFORM UNTIL END-OF-FILE
        PERFORM DISPLAY-A-RECORD
        PERFORM READ-A-RECORD
    END-PERFORM
    CLOSE STUDENT-FILE REPORT-FILE
    STOP RUN.
READ-A-RECORD.
    READ STUDENT-FILE
        AT END MOVE "YES" TO END-OF-FILE-SW
    END-READ.
DISPLAY-A-RECORD.
    MOVE STUDENT-NAME TO STUDENT-NAME-DL
    MOVE STUDENT-ID   TO STUDENT-ID-DL
    WRITE PRINT-RECORD FROM DETAIL-LINE AFTER ADVANCING 1.
```

Index